Praise for The Art of Beeswax

Lisa is truly the Queen Bee when it comes to beeswax candle making and all things hive related. I met Lisa in her early days, and it has been inspiring to watch her knowledge and business grow. Lisa's passion flows through everything she does. Her first book, The Art of Beeswax, is no exception. A comprehensive guide to handling beeswax from start to finish.

—*Colleen Garnsey, Sustainability Consultant in Calgary, Alberta*
HELPS CLIENTS GREEN THEIR EVENTS, WORKSPACES, AND THEIR LIVES

As a novice in the world of beeswax candles, this book has become an invaluable go-to resource. Lisa provides clear instructions, helpful tips, and her enthusiasm for the craft is clearly bee-yond measure, from cover to cover.

—*Joanne Kellough, Wanna-bee Candlemaker*
BEE-AUTY IS IN THE EYE OF THE BEE-HOLDER

I have always been curious about beeswax and candle making. This book has answered all my questions, and I have learned so much. As an educator, I appreciate how the step-by-step instructions have been clearly explained with images added as a guide. I particularly love the "tips" that will save me time and from making many errors. A must-have book for novices or those curious about beeswax candle making! Brava!

—*Joanne Sampson*

Lisa has done the analytical work to simplify beeswax candle making for anyone. A well thought out and delightful exploration of her experience, passion, and testing to make it easier for you. Well done, Lisa! A great addition for the budding candle maker.

—*Nancy Lowery, Founder at The Natural Leader*

This book is a gem for anyone venturing into the world of beeswax candle making. From understanding the materials to creating beautiful candles, it's a journey filled with knowledge and joy. A must-have on the shelf.

—*Kelli Novak, Bee Conservancy Enthusiast*

**THE ART OF BEESWAX © 2024 BY LISA GRAHAM.
ALL RIGHTS RESERVED.**

Published by Author Academy Elite
PO Box 43, Powell, OH 43065
www.AuthorAcademyElite.com

All rights reserved. This book contains material protected under international and federal copyright laws and treaties. Any unauthorized reprint or use of this material is prohibited. No part of this book may be reproduced or transmitted in any form or by any means, electronic or mechanical, including photocopying, recording, or by any information storage and retrieval system, without express written permission from the author.

Identifiers:
LCCN: 2023923251
ISBN: 979-8-88583-289-2 (paperback)
ISBN: 979-8-88583-290-8 (hardback)
ISBN: 979-8-88583-291-5 (ebook)

Available in paperback, hardback, and e-book

Any Internet addresses (websites, blogs, etc.) printed in this book are offered as a resource. They are not intended in any way to be or imply an endorsement by Author Academy Elite, nor does Author Academy Elite vouch for the content of these sites and numbers for the life of this book

Table of Contents

Preface	8
Acknowledgments	9

SECTION 1: MATERIALS — 11

Chapter 1: Beeswax — 11
- Manufacturing Process of Different Waxes — 12
  - Paraffin Wax — 12
  - Gel Wax — 12
  - Vegetable Waxes *(such as soy, palm, and coconut)* — 12
  - Beeswax — 13
- Manufacturing in a Nutshell — 13
- Why Beeswax? — 14
- Where Does Beeswax Come From? — 14
  - Quality and Use in the Hive — 14
  - Color — 15
  - Harvesting and Rendering — 15
    - Rendering — 15
- Uses for Candle Making — 16
  - Beeswax Sheets — 16
  - Melted Beeswax — 16
    - Temperature Sensitivity — 16
    - Material Sensitivity — 17
- Bloom — 17

Chapter 2: Wick — 19
- Types of Wick — 20
  - Cotton Square Braid — 20
    - Square Braid Wick Sizes — 20
    - Does Braid Direction Matter? — 20
  - Pre-Tabbed — 21
    - Creating Your Own — 21
- Wicking Weird Shapes — 21
- Wick Priming — 21
  - Do All Wicks Need to Be Primed? — 22

Chapter 3: Containers — 25
- Selecting a Container — 26
  - Can It Withstand Heat? — 26
  - Test, Test, Test! — 26
- Protect the Surface — 27

Chapter 4: Molds — 29
- Types of Molds — 30
- How Beeswax Behaves — 30
  - Interactions with Different Molding Material — 30
    - Metal — 30
    - Plastic — 30
    - Silicone — 30
  - Mold Removal — 31
- Making Your Own Mold — 31

Chapter 5: Melting Pots — 33

Chapter 6: Double Boiler — 35
- How to Make a Double Boiler — 36
  - Safety Notes — 36
- Tips and Tricks — 36

Chapter 7: Dyes — 39
- Natural Dyes — 40
  - Availability of Materials — 40
- Synthetic Dyes — 40
  - How Dyes Interact with Beeswax — 41
  - How Dyes Affect Wick — 41

Chapter 8: Scents — 43
- Essential Oils — 44
  - Blends — 44
  - Flash Point — 44
  - Potency and Scent Throw — 44
- Fragrance Oils — 45
  - Blends — 45
  - Flash Point — 45
  - Potency and Scent Throw — 45

Table of Contents

SECTION 2: CANDLE MAKING — 47
Chapter 9: Safety — 47
- Cutting Tools — 48
  - Tips and Tricks — 48
- Hot Water and Steam — 48
  - Tips and Tricks — 48
- Melting Vats — 48
  - Tips and Tricks — 48
- Hot Wax — 48
  - Tips and Tricks — 48

Chapter 10: Rolled Beeswax Candles — 51
- Tapers — 52
  - Mini Tapers — 54
  - Flat Top Tapers — 56
  - Spiral Tapers — 58
  - Pencil Tapers — 60
  - Fun Variations — 63
- Pillars — 64
  - Simple Pillar — 66
  - Fun Variations — 69
- Beehive — 72
  - Fun Variations — 75

Chapter 11: Dipped Beeswax Candles — 77
- Materials — 78
  - Melting Vat — 78
  - Binder Clips — 78
  - Weight — 79
- Dipped Candles — 79
  - Birthday Candles — 81
  - Standard Tapers — 81
  - Things to Watch For — 82
  - Fun Variations — 82

Chapter 12: Poured Beeswax Candles — 85
- Tealights — 87
  - Simple Tealight — 88
    - Things to Watch For — 90
- Votives — 93
  - Simple Votive — 94
    - Things to Watch For — 95
- Pillars — 97
  - Simple Pillar — 98
    - Things to Watch For — 101
- Containers — 103
  - Mason Jar Candle — 104
    - Things to Watch For — 105
  - Teacup Candle — 106
    - Things to Watch For — 107
  - Fun Variations — 107

Chapter 13: Adding Dye — 109
- White Beeswax vs Yellow Beeswax — 110
- Creating a New Color — 110
  - Materials — 110
  - Instructions — 110
- Wick and Dye — 111
- Layering Colors — 111
- Things to Watch For — 111
- Tips and Tricks — 111

Chapter 14: Adding Scent — 113
- Essential Oils — 114
- Fragrance Oils — 114
- Creating a New Oil Blend — 114
  - Materials — 115
  - Instructions — 115
  - Things to Watch For — 115
  - Tips and Tricks — 115

SECTION 3: TROUBLESHOOTING & TESTING — 117
Chapter 15: Troubleshooting — 117
- Cracking — 118
  - What is it? — 118
  - Why does it happen? — 118
  - How do I fix it? — 118

Table of Contents

Shrinkage	118
What is it?	118
Why does it happen?	118
How do I fix it?	118
Visible Rings	119
What is it?	119
Why does it happen?	119
How do I fix it?	119
Chapter 16: Testing	**121**
Preparing for a Test	122
Conducting a Test	122
Interpreting the Test Results	124
Verifying the Test	125
Calculating Burn Time	125
Full Burn Calculation	125
Partial Burn Calculation	125
SECTION 4: THE FINISHING TOUCH	**129**
Chapter 17: Creative Candles	**129**
Add More Wax	130
Transfer Candles	130
Pressed Flowers or Other Add-Ons	131
Carved Candles	131
Painted Candles	131
Chapter 18: Gift and Packaging Ideas	**133**
Single Candles	134
Gift Sets	134
Complementary Gift Sets	135
Gift Extras	135
Final Thoughts	135
APPENDIX A: Does the direction of the V in square braid wick affect burn behavior in dipped taper candles?	**138**
Hypothesis	138
Procedure	138
Data	138
Burn Test 1 (0-2 Hours Burn Time)	140
Burn Test 2 (2-4 Hours Burn Time)	142
Burn Test 3 (4-6 Hours Burn Time)	144
Results	146
Summary	149
Quantitative Data	149
Qualitative Data	149
Conclusion	149
Limitations	149
APPENDIX B: Does priming square braid wick affect burn behavior in dipped taper candles?	**150**
Hypothesis	150
Procedure	150
Data	150
Burn Test 1 (0-2 Hours Burn Time)	152
Burn Test 2 (2-4 Hours Burn Time)	154
Burn Test 3 (4-6 Hours Burn Time)	156
Results	158
Summary	161
Quantitative Data	161
Qualitative Data	161
Conclusion	161
Limitations	161
Bibliography	163
About the Author	165
Unleash Your Creativity Course	166
Join our Beeswax Community	167
Custom Beeswax Workshops	168
Our Creator Starter Pack	169
All Materials Now Available	170

Index of Tables

Table 1: Solid Dyes vs Liquid Dyes — 40
Table 2: Sample Testing Table for Wicks — 124
Table 3: Candle Specifications Before Starting Tests — 139
Table 4: Burn Behavior for Burn Test 1 — 140
Table 5: Candle Height and Weight Prior to Burn Test 2 — 142
Table 6: Burn Behavior for Burn Test — 142
Table 7: Candle Height and Weight Prior to Burn Test 3 — 144
Table 8: Burn Behavior for Burn — 144
Table 9: Final Candle Height and Weight — 146
Table 10: Change in Height and Weight for Conditions V Open to Bottom and V Open to Top — 148
Table 11: Candle Specifications Before Starting Tests — 151
Table 12: Burn Behavior for Burn Test 1 — 152
Table 13: Candle Height and Weight Prior to Burn Test 2 — 154
Table 14: Burn Behavior for Burn Test 2 — 154
Table 15: Candle Height and Weight Prior to Burn Test 3 — 156
Table 16: Burn Behavior for Burn Test 3 — 156
Table 17: Final Candle Height and Weight — 158
Table 18: Change in Height and Weight for Primed Wick and Unprimed Wick — 160

Table of Figures

Figure 1: Height Changes Over Time for V Open to Bottom — 146
Figure 2: Height Changes Over Time for V Open to Top — 147
Figure 3: Weight Changes Over Time for V Open to Bottom — 147
Figure 4: Weight Changes Over Time for V Open to Top — 148
Figure 5: Height Changes Over Time for Primed Wick — 158
Figure 6: Height Changes Over Time for Unprimed Wick — 159
Figure 7: Weight Changes Over Time for Primed Wick — 159
Figure 8: Weight Changes Over Time for Unprimed Wick — 163

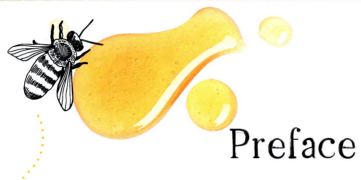

Preface

The inspiration for this book arose from my challenges as a new beeswax candle maker—it was nearly impossible to find useful information on creating beeswax candles. Many books cover beeswax candle making in a small section with other waxes as the focus, or the book includes beeswax candles along with how to make other beeswax products.

As I progressed in my beeswax candle making journey, I found more to learn! Many tips and tricks were learned through trial and error. A scientifically minded person, I was curious to delve deeper into the science behind the materials used. What an adventure! I'm constantly sharing small parts of my knowledge in workshops and with those who purchase products at YYC Beeswax and The Abelo Collection. In this book, I share over a decade of practical experience and research on making candles with beeswax.

In this book, I share over a decade of practical experience and research on making candles with beeswax.

This book would not be possible without the help and support of many people.

Acknowledgments

Writing is a lonely endeavor, and this book would not be possible without the help and support of many people. Thank you to Mia for helping with some of the testing and providing feedback on the book. Thank you to my partner Sergio for putting up with hours of writing, testing, editing, and requests for input. Thank you to friends and family for your continued support on my beeswax adventures - Marla, Doug, Justin, Nathan, Joan, Garry, Donna, Carol, Emma, Karlie, Mike, Sandy, Carmen, George, Susan, Joe, Marie, John, Gord, John, Shahin, Michael, Ina, Mike, Aubrey, Trevor, Marloes, David, Lucie, Kelli, Miro, Lily, Joanne, Donna, Brad, Nancy, Andy, Dave, Van, Kyle, Kat, Reece, Echo, and so many more. Thank you to everyone involved in bringing the final stages of this book together is such a beautiful way-Celina for the graphic design; Joanne, and Nancy, and Sergio for editing suggestions; and Author Academy Elite for helping to bring this book to the world.

Beeswax

To remove the remaining particles, the wax is re-melted and put through filters of increasingly smaller size. From there, the wax is ready to use in candles.

CHAPTER 1
Beeswax

Not all waxes are created equal. From paraffin to beeswax (of course!), the choice of wax plays a crucial role in the candle's aesthetics, burn time, and environmental impact. Let's explore how four different waxes commonly used in candle making are produced.

Section 1: Materials

Manufacturing Process of Different Waxes

Paraffin Wax

Paraffin wax is derived from petroleum, coal, or shale. It starts out as what's called a slack wax, which is a by-product of manufacturing lubricating oils.

Once the slack wax is obtained, the oils need to be removed. This is commonly done by heating the wax, mixing it with a solvent, and allowing it to cool. On cooling, the wax and the oil are separated. This leaves a solid wax with some solvent and a liquid oil with some solvent. This is filtered down to the wax/solvent mix.

At this stage, the wax goes through a distillation process. The distillation removes the remaining solvent using a steam-heated kettle. The result of this stage is a product wax ready for further refining.

The next step in the process results in a fully refined wax. To get to this state, the product wax is passed through a bed of clay that removes color. It is also passed through a vacuum-stripping tower, which removes odors.

Gel Wax

Gel wax is a petroleum-derived wax with a unique gel-like consistency. It is created by polymerizing mineral oil and polymer resin.

Polymerization is a chemical process where small molecules (monomers) come together to form long-chain polymers.

Once polymerization is complete, the gel wax is ready for use in candle making.

Vegetable Waxes (such as soy, palm, and coconut)

First, let's see where each type of wax comes from:

- Soy wax—derived from the oil of soybeans. The process starts by harvesting soybeans. From there, the beans are washed, split, de-hulled, and turned into flakes. Next, the oil is removed.

- Palm wax—derived from the fruit of oil palm trees. The oil is removed from the fruit and kernel through pressing and clarified to remove impurities.

- Coconut wax – derived from the oil naturally found in coconuts. The process starts by cold pressing the oil out of the meat of coconuts.

After the oil is removed, it goes through a hydrogenation process. Hydrogenation is a chemical reaction between molecular hydrogen and an element or compound usually in the presence of a catalyst. In the case of soy, molecular hydrogen, soybean oil (element or compound), and often nickel (catalyst) are present.

Once hydrogenation is complete, the characteristics of the wax have changed. The melting point is different, and it is solid at room temperature. Now, it's ready for use in candles.

Beeswax

Beeswax is an insect-made wax. It is secreted from the wax glands of the honey bee.

Beeswax is one of the main building materials in the beehive. It can be harvested along with honey. Directly from the hive, beeswax may contain dirt, grass, honey, bee parts, and other contaminants.

There are two steps in the process to convert beeswax into a material suitable for candle making:

1. Rendering
2. Filtering

Rendering is often done using water to remove honey and separate the wax from some particles. The wax and water are heated until the wax melts. The wax is allowed to cool and removed. Heavy particles will drop to the bottom of the container, and honey will dissolve in water. However, some particles will still remain in the wax.

To remove the remaining particles, the wax is re-melted and put through filters of increasingly smaller size. From there, the wax is ready to use in candles.

Manufacturing in a Nutshell

Each wax has different pros and cons. In the candle-making world, different waxes may also be combined to achieve specific results. Things quickly start to get complicated!

Beeswax is sensitive to changes in temperature and can burn if direct heat is applied to it.

Why Beeswax?

I believe the choice of candle-making materials is highly personal. Here is a list of what draws me to beeswax:

- Fascination with bees—my first exposure to beeswax was working with bees as a summer job. Here in Canada, we are unable to work with bees all year, and it's nice to have a reminder of summer days gone by and to look forward to the new season.
- Scent—I love the smell of a healthy beehive. Although there is more than just beeswax contributing to the unique hive scent, beeswax reminds me of the joy of working with the bees in the summer.
- Color and feel—winter nights are long, and burning a beautiful yellow beeswax candle reminds me of sunny summer days. I also find the flame of a beeswax candle warmer more soothing than other candles (probably my imagination, but oh well!).
- The challenge—beeswax can be a challenging medium with which to work. Every day, I am learning something new to improve what I'm already doing.
- Simplicity—although it can be a challenge to work with beeswax, I love the simplicity of working with a single material and seeing how many uses I can find for it.

In summary, it's emotional! For me, beeswax evokes nostalgia and feelings of warmth and comfort. With different life experiences, perhaps I would have picked a different medium for candle making!

Where Does Beeswax Come From?

Beeswax is produced by honey bees (genus Apis). Special wax glands on the abdomen secrete scales of wax 1–2mm in diameter. The bees then soften the scales and work them into the existing comb.[i] Once the comb is built, it is used for brood rearing and food storage (honey and pollen).[ii]

Quality and Use in the Hive

Over time, the wax darkens as it is used by the bees and impurities are introduced. For example, wax used for brood may contain cocoon material, propolis, and pollen residue.[iii] The highest-quality wax comes from cappings. This wax is used to seal cells of ripe honey. It is clean and light in color, making it highly desirable for crafting.[iv]

Color

Newly created beeswax is nearly white in color. Over time, impurities are introduced into the wax, primarily from pollen causing it to change color. The color varies based on the types of pollen the bees are bringing into the hive and the properties of the pollen. Some types of pollen will color the wax, while others will not. In order to remove coloring from the wax, beeswax can be put through a chemical or charcoal filtration process, returning it to white! That said, it is still completely usable as yellow wax, provided it has been sufficiently filtered.

Harvesting and Rendering

Beeswax is harvested with honey. When the honey is removed from the hive, beeswax and other bits of miscellany are mixed together.

The honey is filtered off, leaving a mixture of wax, some honey, and other particles. The transformation of this remaining mixture into usable beeswax is known as rendering.

Although we won't cover this topic in depth here, it is useful to have a general understanding of the process used for producing beeswax. Through this, you gain an appreciation for the labor involved as well as understand the differences in beeswax available on the market today. You can then make an informed decision when purchasing your crafting material.

Rendering

RENDER (VERB): MELT DOWN IN ORDER TO CLARIFY IT.[IV]

After the honey is removed, the remaining mixture of beeswax, honey, and other particles is refined further. The general process is as follows:

1. Melt down beeswax mixture in water.
2. Separate beeswax from debris.
3. Filter beeswax through a fine filter to capture remaining debris.

Filtration can be done as many times as necessary to achieve the desired purity of wax.

At this point, the beeswax is ready for use. It's extremely important in candle making to use well-filtered beeswax, as debris can affect the way your candles burn (for example by clogging the wick).[vii]

Beeswax sheets can be used in both beekeeping and crafting.

Uses for Candle Making

This book will cover two methods to use beeswax in candle making—beeswax sheets for rolled candles and melted beeswax for poured and dipped candles. Section 2 starts with rolled candles, as I find they make an excellent introduction to candle making. They are easy to make, and you don't need many special supplies to get started.

Beeswax Sheets

Beeswax sheets can be used in both beekeeping and crafting. Beekeepers can use beeswax sheets to provide a template for the bees and give them a head start on building out new frames. Getting them started with a wax base means less work for the bees to build, which can translate into more honey. To start, a frame is crisscrossed with wires. The beeswax sheet is gently heated until it melts into the wires on the frame.

From here, the frame is ready to go into a beehive! The wire on the frame provides stability for the wax, as the temperature in the hive can cause the wax sheet to bend if the wires aren't in place. Bent sheets can cause challenges for a beekeeper managing the hive by making it more difficult to remove frames easily during hive checks.

In terms of crafting, it doesn't take much to transform a beeswax sheet into a usable candle. By cutting and rolling, you can have a candle ready to burn in less than half an hour. These candles require minimal equipment to get started and create minimal mess. They also make an ideal craft for children, as they can get creative without the safety hazards of using hot wax. Chapter 10 covers a few examples of different candles you can make with beeswax sheets.

Melted Beeswax

The setup for creating candles from melted beeswax is more elaborate than using beeswax sheets. Using melted wax introduces burn hazards and gets quite messy!

Temperature Sensitivity

Beeswax is sensitive to changes in temperature, and if the wax gets too hot, the wax may darken, and scent can be compromised.[viii] When melting beeswax, I recommend using a double boiler, which heats the wax more gently. Since beeswax is comprised of a number of different components—each of which have a different melting point—beeswax has an interesting staged melting profile. Beeswax begins to melt at around 61–63°C (142–145°F) and is completely liquid at 64–66°C (147–151°F).[ix]

Material Sensitivity

It's also important to consider the type of materials used as a container for melting beeswax. Certain metals—such as steel, aluminum, zinc, and copper—can discolor the wax.[x] Stainless steel does not discolor wax, and this is what I like to use. More information on this can be found in Chapter 5.

Bloom

Bloom (or efflorescence) is a natural phenomenon. It manifests as a light matte film, which may appear blotchy on the surface of beeswax. This film is made up of unsaturated hydrocarbons or linear alkenes.[xi] In a finished product, bloom can be left alone or removed for a time through gentle heating. In cases of darkly dyed wax, it may be desirable to remove bloom to restore the vibrancy of the dye.

Bloom is less noticeable in lightly colored wax. The main difference is a matte appearance (with bloom) or slightly shiny (without bloom). Bloom will recur over time. Exposure to cool temperatures can accelerate the process as the unsaturated hydrocarbons crystallize more quickly.[xii]

Candle with bloom | Bloom removed

Bloom will recur over time. Exposure to cool temperatures accelerates the process.

Wick

Wicking is one of the big challenges in making great beeswax candles.

CHAPTER 2
Wick

Wicking is one of the big challenges in making great beeswax candles. There are many wick options available, and it can get a bit confusing. This chapter looks at some of the wicks I've used. Since beeswax varies slightly in composition, it's important to spot check your wicking once in a while after you've determined the correct wick size for your candles. The key to finding the correct wick is to test, test, test! Once you've chosen your wicks and created your candles, be sure to read through Chapter 16, which has some tips on how to test your candles and what to look for.

There are five major types of wicks: flat, square, cored, wooden, and specialty.

In each chapter, I'll provide wick recommendations based on my experimentation. These are meant to give you a starting point—you may need to increase or decrease the wick size, as your beeswax may give you different burn results. If you are using a different type of wick, you'll have to experiment as well!

Types of Wick

There are a TON of different types of wicks available for candles. I primarily use cotton square braid and pre-tabbed wicks for my candles. I have known others to try hemp, wood wicks, string, and various other materials. Square braid and pre-tabbed work well for me, so that's what I tended to stick with as a beginner anyway!

According to candles.org, there are five major types of wicks: flat, square, cored, wooden, and specialty.[xiii]

Cotton Square Braid

Cotton square braid wicks are often sold in long lengths (spools or by the meter or foot). This makes them very easy to cut to size for your project. As the candle burns, the wicks curl in the flame. This particular type of wick is great for beeswax, as it helps prevent wick clogging.[xiv]

Square Braid Wick Sizes

There are many different sizes of square braid wick, and it can be tricky to remember how the size changes with the different types. In general, the larger the number on its own, the larger the wick (wick size 2 is bigger than wick size 1). The larger the number when paired with a 0, the smaller the wick (wick size 5/0 is smaller than 1/0). An easy trick I use to remember the difference is to think of the /0 wicks as being negative numbers—the bigger the negative number, the further away from 0, which means the smaller it gets! This handy chart is also helpful:[xv]

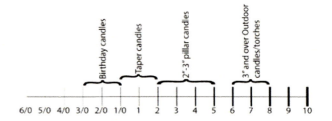

Square Braid Wick Sizes

Does Braid Direction Matter?

Looking carefully at square braid wick, you will notice a subtle V pattern on certain sides of the wick. Does the direction of this V actually matter? If so, what does it do?

I conducted a small experiment to test whether the direction of the braid is important for the burn behavior of the candle. The experiment showed no significant difference in the quantitative burn behavior, but the candles with the V open to the top mushroomed less (see Chapter 16 for information on mushrooming). If you're curious about the full experiment, take a look at Appendix A. Note that the experiment was done using dipped taper candle, so there is more testing to do with other types of candles and to validate the data with a larger experiment.

As with any wick testing, this requires a bit of trial and error to get it to burn exactly how you'd like.

Pre-tabbed

Pre-tabbed wicks are stiffer wicks that I like to use for container candles, votives, and tealights. These wicks contain a core that helps keep the wick upright as the candle is burning. Core components may include paper, cotton, zinc, or tin.[xvi] My personal preference is paper filament wicks, as the metal components can be a cause for concern for some people. I love using pre-tabbed wicks because they are pre-primed (the wick is soaked in wax to remove air bubbles) and ready to go right out of the package.

Creating Your Own

For some instances, pre-tabbed wicks don't come in the right size for the candle you're making. In this case, I create my own tabbed wick using wick tabs and cotton square braid wick of the appropriate size. First, I cut a piece of wick to size. Then I prime the wick (see the section Wick Priming later in this chapter). Finally, I thread the primed wick through the hole in the tab and tighten the exposed metal tabs with pliers to anchor the wick. Once this process is done, I use the wick as I would any other pre-tabbed wick. Creating a tabbed wick in this manner is a bit flimsier than purchased pre-tabbed wicks because the cotton braid wick does not have the core found in pre-tabbed wicks.

Wicking Weird Shapes

There are a lot of very interesting molds available in odd shapes. My method of approaching these candles is to decide what I consider a good burn experience with the candle (how much wax should be left over in an ideal burn? Should it be designed to tunnel, leaving the outside shape intact for later use with battery powered candles, as a decoration, or with other candles such as tealights? How quickly or slowly should it burn?) and wick accordingly.

When I was starting, I stuck with mostly straight candles so I could understand how different wick sizes behaved. I used this information along with what I wanted to create in the burn experience to choose a wick for different shaped candles. This provided a starting point from which I could decide if the wicking was correct, or if it needed a larger or smaller wick. As with any wick testing, this requires a bit of trial and error to get it to burn exactly how you'd like.

Wick Priming

Priming a wick involves soaking the wick in liquid wax until no more air bubbles rise to the surface. This is a very handy process to use if you are making your own pre-tabbed wicks (as mentioned earlier in this chapter).

Priming a wick is very simple:

1. Select the length of wick you'd like to prime.
2. Hold one end of the wick and lower it into hot wax.
3. Hold the wick in place allowing it to soak until no more air bubbles rise to the surface.

If you would like to leave the top part of the wick unprimed, you are finished!

If you would like to prime the entire length of the wick, it can be helpful to prime it in two stages.

Wick priming removes air bubbles from wicks.

Follow the steps above with the following changes:
1. Soak one half of the wick as outlined above.
2. Allow the soaked half to cool until it can be handled.
3. Holding the soaked half of the wick, soak the other half of the wick as outlined above.

This will keep your fingers clean, and you won't have to go fishing for the wick at the bottom of your melting vat!

Do All Wicks Need to Be Primed?

When I was starting, some sources suggested wicks to be primed while others did not. I put together another experiment to test whether priming was important for dipped tapers. The results showed priming does not make a measurable difference in the burn behavior of tapers. There is still more testing to do on other types of candles such as pillars and to validate this data with a larger experiment.

For the full experiment, see Appendix B

Containers

The most important part about selecting a container for your beeswax candles is to ensure it can withstand the heat.

CHAPTER 3
Containers

Is it really true that beeswax can be used as a container candle? I say a wholehearted YES to this! The first beeswax container candles I made were tealights, and I've since tried everything from glass jars to teacups.

Selecting a Container

There are many different types of containers made from a variety of materials that work well for beeswax candles.

Can it Withstand Heat?

The most important part about selecting a container for your beeswax candles is to ensure it can withstand the heat. I like using mason jars because they are designed to withstand canning temperatures, which get much hotter than burning beeswax.

I also like using teacups and coffee mugs for the same reason; however, when I'm using teacups, I'm very careful about checking for cracks. I also haven't been brave enough to try some of the very thin china cups I've come across either. (They are made in Japan with stunning hand painting, and I really want to use them to drink out of instead!)

Pottery makes a great vessel for container candles as well.

The key here is to get creative and move on to the next step... testing!

Test, Test, Test!

To check if a container will work with beeswax, I do a test run. Since I use a wide variety of different containers, it's not feasible to test every container, so I try to buy containers in groups. For example, I found some beautiful tall glasses that would fit a votive-sized candle. Although I wasn't sure they would work, I bought a dozen, figuring I could reuse, repurpose, or sell them if they didn't work.

Similarly for teacups, I buy similar weight china in similar sizes so I don't have to constantly re-test for heat resistance and wick size.

As a precaution, I like to create a special testing environment when I'm testing new containers in case the container breaks. I place a large sheet of aluminum foil over my heat-resistant surface with the edges folded up (pictured below). I like to use aluminum foil because it is easy to form the edges and it's readily available in my work area (more on this later!).

This way, if the container breaks, the wax will be contained, and it doesn't make a huge mess! If you end up with a broken container, be sure to safely dispose of all components—recovered bits of wax may end up with parts of your broken container, so it's safer to dispose of the entire experiment.

Protect the Surface

I always burn container candles on a heat-resistant surface such as a coaster, hot pad, or trivet to protect the surface on which the candle is burning.

Some container candles may burn without damaging the surface, but I don't like to take that risk!

I place a large sheet of aluminum foil over my heat-resistant surface with the edges folded up.

Molds

So far, I've come across three main types of molds — metal, plastic, and silicone.

CHAPTER 4
Molds

Molds are a fun way to add some incredibly creative shapes and designs to your candle repertoire.

Types of Molds

So far, I've come across three main types of molds—metal, plastic, and silicone.

How Beeswax Behaves

With different types of mold material, beeswax behaves a little differently.

Interactions with Different Molding Material

METAL

Most of the time, I've found metal molds work very well with beeswax.

I use metal pillar and votive molds and find the wax separates enough from the edges for easy removal.

However, sometimes the wax ends up sticking to the side, so I end up fixing or remaking the candle. I don't use mold release. I tried it in my early candle making days and didn't notice a difference with the molds I used. Most of my molds are very simple shapes, so perhaps I will try it again if I need to make something more detailed.

PLASTIC

Although I generally avoid plastic molds, I have tried them a couple times. My initial experiences were similar to the metal molds. I allowed the wax to cool completely (left overnight), and they were easy to remove from the mold. I have not tested them extensively enough to speak to durability and long term use.

SILICONE

I've found silicone heats up and cools down with the beeswax, so the wax doesn't shrink away from the sides as with other mold materials. My favorite silicone molds have walls that are thin and flexible

enough to work the candle out but not too thin that they break. Depending on the design, molds with thick walls can be a challenge to work with—I've found if the walls are too thick, it can be hard on the hands to get the candles out. (More on that later where I share my mold-making experiences.)

Mold Removal

Beeswax shrinks as it cools, allowing it to come out of your mold easily most of the time. I don't use mold release on my molds and rarely run into any issues. That said, sometimes the candle is a little stubborn, or I get impatient and try to take the candle out while it's still too warm. Some of the tricks I've used to get stubborn candles out of molds:

- Run the mold under cold water or place it in an ice bath. (This is not my preferred method because it can take a LOT of water!)

- Put the mold in the freezer (or outside if it's cold).

- Leave the mold overnight.

- If all else fails, I'll use a heat gun on metal molds. I try to avoid this because it can end up melting the candle. I often end up redoing candles I've removed using heat.

Making Your Own Mold

Once you get the hang of using other molds, it's a fun process to create your own mold. I like using silicone mold kits for my designs.

For my first silicone mold-making experience, I was creating custom dyed birthday candles with a hexagon pattern. In creating the mold, I placed the negatives too far apart, leading to very thick mold walls. It's quite hard on the hands to make a lot of these candles because they are a bit of a challenge to remove from the mold due to the wall thickness.

Metal molds can become very hot during the pouring process, so handle them with care using heat-resistant gloves or mitts.

Melting Pots

Containers made from steel, aluminum, zinc, and copper can cause beeswax to darken; however, stainless steel is fine to use.

CHAPTER 5
Melting Pots

As mentioned in Chapter 1, the materials in the container used for melting beeswax is important! Certain types of metals can cause the beeswax to discolor.

Containers made from steel, aluminum, zinc, and copper can cause beeswax to darken; however, stainless steel is fine to use.[xvii]

For materials other than metal, I've picked up old ceramic cream dishes because they have a great pouring spout. These are great to get started with. I have two containers I've been using for over eight years with no issues. However, these can break from the constant heat by using them in a double boiler. I plan to replace mine with stainless steel pots as they become unusable. The majority of containers I use now are stainless steel milk frothing/gravy jugs. I love the handle and find the spout pours well.

Double Boiler

Beeswax should be melted using a double boiler.

CHAPTER 6
Double Boiler

Beeswax should be melted using a double boiler. You are welcome to use a true double boiler setup or create your own. In this chapter, I'll outline the process of creating your own double boiler.

How to Make a Double Boiler

These instructions are based on easily found materials. Feel free to get creative!

MATERIALS

- Old pot (I recommend setting aside this pot exclusively for crafting. It will get messy! If you don't have an old pot on hand, try a second-hand store.)
- River rocks (These can be purchased at select dollar stores, or you can find them yourself outside. I like to use flat stones as it helps keep the melting pot level.), small cooling rack (this will lift the melting pot off the bottom and is already level.), or something else
- Melting pot (See Chapter 5 for suggestions)
- Water

INSTRUCTIONS

1. Place the rocks evenly in the bottom of the pot. Try to keep the layer of rocks even so your melting pot is stable.

2. Place your melting pot on the rocks and put some beeswax in the pot. (This is optional but will help prevent the pot from tipping when we add the water in the next step.)

3. Add water to the pot. You want enough water to heat the sides of the melting pot but not so much that the melting pot floats. (It's a bit of a nightmare to get the water out of the beeswax if it tips into the water!)
4. Put your pot on the stove and turn on the heat!

SAFETY

When making your own double boiler, you are working with hot wax, hot water, and steam. It is very easy to get a steam burn if you're not paying attention or for hot water to bubble up if the heat is too high. Make sure you're focused on your project!

The rocks are used to prevent air pockets from forming under your melting pot. By putting your melting pot directly on the bottom of the pot, you run the risk of trapping air underneath, which can bubble up, overturning your melting vat, or possibly exploding, leading to possible injury (and a definite mess)!

TIPS AND TRICKS

I like to create a special crafting space when working with the double boiler.

Putting a drop cloth on the floor and aluminum foil under a portable burner will save you lots of clean up time!

Dyes

It's important to note that dyes will interact with the natural color of beeswax.

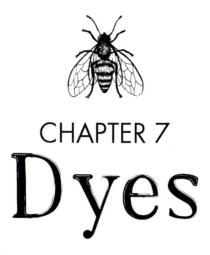

CHAPTER 7
Dyes

Dyes come in a few different shapes and forms. Which dyes you choose to use will depend on what you find easy to work with to give you the results you want.

Sediment left over at the end of a naturally dyed wax batch

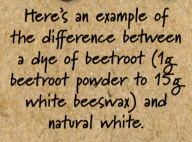

Here's an example of the difference between a dye of beetroot (1g beetroot powder to 15g white beeswax) and natural white.

On the bottom of the block of dyed wax, you can see the sediment.

Natural Dyes

Natural dyes can enhance your beeswax candles if you're looking for a more muted color palette. I tend to stay away from natural dyes in most cases because they can be very difficult to use. I've found that it takes a lot of material to get minimal color change, and there is often a lot of sediment left over at the end.

Here's an example of a tealight I tested using beetroot powder. Notice how it shows up as ombre from the top to the bottom of the candle. The top is very light, and the bottom shows where sediment has settled.

Availability of Materials

Natural dyes can be very attractive in that you can readily make them yourself—beet root powder can be made with beets grown from your garden, you can get new life from onion skins, and you can try your hand at making other dyes from material readily available in your area.

The top is very light, and the bottom shows where sediment has settled.

Synthetic Dyes

Synthetic dyes tend to provide more color variety, vibrancy, and better consistency across batches when using white beeswax. They are highly concentrated pigments available in solid or liquid form. I find solid-form dyes more easily available, so that's what I use. Here's a handy chart that outlines the different characteristics of each type of dye:

Table 1: Solid Dyes vs Liquid Dyes

SOLID DYE	LIQUID DYE
Form is solid chips/blocks or powder	Form is liquid
Works well for light to dark colors	Works well for light to medium colors
May have some sediment when dissolved and mixed	Sediment-free
Estimated 30 g (~1oz) of chips in 16 kg (~35 lbs) of wax for a medium shade*	Estimated 30 g (~1 oz) liquid in 45 kg (~100 lbs) of wax for a medium shade*

* This is a very rough estimate. Your results will vary based on the supplier you choose for dyes and the wax you are using. Many dye manufacturers will provide some guidelines on how much dye you will need for a certain amount of wax to achieve a certain color intensity. I've found they often focus on soy or paraffin wax for these recommendations, which both behave differently than beeswax. My personal experiences are shared below. Experimenting is key!

How Dyes Interact with Beeswax

It's important to note that dyes will interact with the natural color of beeswax. I've tried creating colors in the past that look great when first poured but turn pretty ugly as they cool and as they age.

Here's an example of a failed and successful green dye experiment:

The green on the left was initially a green I was quite happy with but did not age well. The green on the right, however, was the final recipe I settled on and seems to hold up well!

My preference is to use white beeswax for most dyeing, although I have found you can get away with yellow wax if you're creating some very dark colors (such as black)!

How Dyes Affect Wick

I've found that dyeing may require a wick size adjustment, especially for dark colors. It's very important to test wick sizes as you create new colors!

scents

Essential oils are created from organic matter such as leaves, stems, flowers, seeds, roots, fruit rinds, resins, and barks.

CHAPTER 8
Scents

Although beeswax has its own unique and lovely scent, sometimes it's nice to add something a little different. Whether it's for practical use (such as aromatherapy or bug management), evoking a treasured memory, or just for fun, adding scent can be an enjoyable experiment to try.

It's important to note that not all scents work well with beeswax! Since beeswax already has its own aroma, it's important to take that into account when choosing a scent. I tried a cherry musk scent once that was a good idea in theory but absolutely awful in execution. (Or perhaps it's because I'm not a huge musk fan to begin with!)

> Not every fragrance complements beeswax effectively. Considering that beeswax carries its own distinct aroma, it's essential to factor that in when selecting a scent.

Essential Oils

Essential oils are created from organic matter such as leaves, stems, flowers, seeds, roots, fruit rinds, resins, and barks.[xviii] There are many methods for extracting oils from this matter such as hydro-distillation, steam distillation, cold pressing, and so much more. The resulting mixture is a highly concentrated oil.

Prices on essential oils vary based on the type of plant and the method of oil extraction. Different plants have different amounts of essential oil, so for some oils, a lot of plant material is needed to get a small amount of oil. As an example, freshly harvested thyme (thymus vulgaris) yields 0.7–5% oil whereas freshly harvested rose otto (rosa damascena) only yields 0.02–0.03% oil.[xx]

Blends

Essential oils can be purchased individually or as blends. Blends can be purchased or created. If you are creating your own blends, you can get as technical as you'd like. Perfumers work with base, middle, and top notes (there are many resources available if you'd like to learn more on the topic), or you can skip the technical details and go with what smells best to you.

Flash Point

For safety reasons, it's important to know the flash point of the oil you're using. Flash point is the temperature at which the oil will catch fire. When choosing oils, make sure the flash point is much higher than the temperature of the lit candle.

Potency and Scent Throw

Oils differ in potency right out of the bottle and once they are in a candle. Mint, for example, quickly dissociates when exposed to heat, making it less useful as a scent whereas I've found lavender and cinnamon last much longer.

Scent throw also varies among oils. I've found some that smell great when the candle is unlit (called cold throw), but they don't smell much once it's lit (called hot throw). Other candles don't have great cold throw, but turn out to have an amazing hot throw. Still others have good cold and hot throw. This is one of the reasons it's so important to test burn your candles!

Fragrance Oils

Fragrance oils are lab-created (synthetic) or partially lab-created (natural) scents. A synthetic fragrance oil is made in a lab and can result in scents that are impossible to find naturally. Natural fragrance oils, on the other hand, are derived from extracting specific components of a natural complex scent in a lab to highlight certain scent characteristics.

There is quite a variety of fragrances available. It's important to note that some people may have adverse reactions to fragrance oils.

Blends

As with essential oils, fragrance oils can be blended to create new scents.

Flash Point

Similar safety precautions should be taken with fragrance oils as with essential oils.

Potency and Scent Throw

I've found potency and scent throw considerations for fragrance oils very similar to essential oils.

The key—test, test, test!

As with essential oils, fragrance oils can be blended to create new scents.

Safety

When using a double boiler, you are at risk of hot water and steam burns, especially when adding or removing melting vats when the water has been heating for awhile.

CHAPTER 9
Safety

Candle making is not without risk. In the forthcoming chapters, we'll be learning to make various kinds of candles. Each method will come with associated risks. This chapter outlines some of the safety hazards of candle making and how to stay safe on your candle making journey.

Cutting Tools

When making rolled or dipped candles, you will be using scissors and an Exacto knife or something similar. There is a risk of cuts, especially with knives.

TIPS AND TRICKS
- Use a block to elevate your fingers above the knife when you are cutting beeswax sheets.
- Be patient! Cut slowly and deliberately.
- Be aware of your body at all times. Keep fingers out of the path of knives.
- Be aware of other people and pets in the vicinity.
- Instead of an Exacto knife, try using a pizza cutter.
- Cut away from yourself where possible.

Hot Water and Steam

When using a double boiler, you are at risk of hot water and steam burns, especially when adding or removing melting vats when the water has been heating for awhile.

TIPS AND TRICKS
- Keep the temperature as low as you can to prevent excessive boiling while keeping the wax at an appropriate temperature.
- Be aware of hot spots in your double boiler where the water bubbles or excessive steam rises. Avoid these areas.
- Keep your hands and face away from the water and steam as much as possible. If you are removing a melting vat, do so without lingering.
- Ensure any pot handles are safe from bumping. I like to use pots with a double handle as the short handles are less likely to be bumped.

Melting Vats

Melting vats can get very hot when they have been on the heat for a period of time. Removing a hot melting vat without protection for your hands can result in burns.

TIPS AND TRICKS
- Use a dry towel or oven mitts to remove melting vats. If the fabric is wet, it can cause a steam burn.
- Keep handles of melting vats out of hot spots in your double boiler where possible.

Hot Wax

Hot wax can cause burns. I most commonly get hot wax on my shoes, pants, and hands, so I avoid exposing as much skin as possible.

TIPS AND TRICKS
- Wear closed toe shoes to protect your feet.
- Wear long pants to protect your legs.
- Wear long sleeves to protect your arms.
- Be aware of your position and the hot wax. Position yourself away from any potential spills.

It is helpful to have a first aid kit near your work area in case of any accidents.

In case you didn't know, this is the queen bee!

Rolled Beeswax

Rolled candles are one of the easiest candles to make. With minimal supplies, work, and mess, you'll have gorgeous candles before you know it!

CHAPTER 10
Rolled Beeswax Candles

One of the easiest ways to get started, rolled beeswax candles require minimal supplies, space, preparation, and cleanup! They are great for small children as there is no hot wax involved. In this chapter, we will explore three different styles of candles you can make with beeswax sheets and some interesting variations to make your creation stand out.

> Measure twice, cut once. If your taper is too big for its holder, gently mold the bottom of the candle until it fits.

Tapers

Imagine indulging in a fancy dinner by candlelight or reading a book by a fireplace with beautiful tapers burning on the mantle. Perhaps you've seen a movie where one of the characters uses a taper candle to investigate a bump in the night. Tapers are versatile, from adding a touch of elegance to serving a very practical purpose.

Tapers are one of the easiest rolled candles to make. With minimal cutting and measuring, you can have a beautiful result in no time!

SAFETY: Be very careful with knives. Always cut away from yourself and others. Keep your fingers out of the path of the knife!

TIPS AND TRICKS: Measure twice, cut once. If your taper is too big for its holder, gently mold the bottom of the candle until it fits.

Mini Tapers

Mini tapers are the perfect starter project for small children and people with small hands. It's much easier to spread 10 cm (4") than 20 cm (8") or more! Mini tapers will fit in a standard taper holder.

MATERIALS

- 1 – 21.5 x 41.5 cm (8.5 x 16") Sheet of beeswax in the color of your choice
- Wick (approximately 11.5 cm (4.5"))
- Sharp knife (I like to use an Exacto knife)
- Scissors
- Cutting board
- Ruler

INSTRUCTIONS

1. If your sheet of wax has bloom on it or isn't very supple, gently heat it with a hair dryer. Be very careful not to melt it!

2. Place the beeswax sheet on the cutting board with the long edge facing you.

3. Cut the sheet into four equal parts. Each cut piece should measure approximately 21.5 x 10 cm (8.5 x 4").

TIP: I like to mark each edge first, connect the markings with the ruler, and then cut.

4. If you want all your candles to be the same height, stack the four pieces of wax and trim any excess from larger pieces.

5. Set aside three of the pieces you just cut.

6. Cut a piece of wick the length of the short edge of one piece of wax plus a bit extra. I like to run the wick along the short edge of the wax so I can decide how much extra I would like to have coming out of the top.

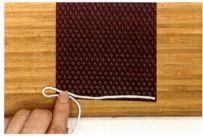

7. Use the piece of wick you just cut as a template to cut three more pieces of wick. Set the extra wick aside.

8. Identify the V shape in the wick. The V will open to the top of your candle. This will help your candles burn better.

9. With the short edge of the wax facing you, align the wick along the edge of the wax, making sure the V shape of the wick is opening at the top of your candle and the wick goes all the way to the bottom of the wax.

10. Gently roll the edge of the wax over the wick.

11. Roll the candle firmly, making sure the bottom stays flat. If it starts to angle too much, simply unroll and re-roll. Try to minimize the unrolling/re-rolling as the wax can start to break apart.

12. Once you have finished rolling, gently press the edge of the wax into the candle. If the bottom isn't quite flat, you can press it into your cutting board to flatten it out.

13. Trim the wick if needed.
14. Repeat steps 8–13 for the remaining three pieces of wax.

Flat Top Tapers

These are the taller version of the mini taper. These candles end up approximately 20 cm (8") tall and make an elegant accent to your dinner table or mantle. These tapers will fit in a standard taper holder.

MATERIALS

- 1 – 21.5 x 41.5 cm (8.5 x 16") Sheet of beeswax in the color of your choice
- Wick (approximately 46 cm (18"))
- Sharp knife (I like to use an Exacto knife)
- Scissors
- Cutting board
- Ruler

INSTRUCTIONS

1. If your sheet of wax has bloom on it or isn't very supple, gently heat it with a hair dryer. Be very careful not to melt it!

2. Place the beeswax sheet on the cutting board with the long edge facing you.

3. Cut the sheet in half. Each cut piece should measure approximately 21.5 x 20 cm (8.5 x 8").

TIP: I like to mark each edge first, connect the markings with the ruler, and then cut.

4. If you want your candles to be the same height, stack the pieces of wax and trim any excess from larger piece.

5. Set aside one of the pieces you just cut.

6. Cut a piece of wick the length of the 20 cm (8") edge of one piece of wax plus a bit extra. I like to run the wick along the short edge of the wax so I can decide how much extra I would like to have coming out of the top.

7. Use the piece of wick you just cut as a template to cut another piece of wick. Set the extra wick aside.

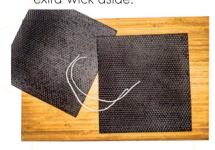

8. Identify the V shape in the wick. The V will open to the top of your candle. This will help your candles burn better.

9. With the short edge of the wax facing you, align the wick along the edge of the wax, making sure the V shape of the wick is opening at the top of your candle, and the wick goes all the way to the bottom of the wax.

10. Gently roll the edge of the wax over the wick.

11. Roll the candle firmly, making sure the bottom stays flat. If it starts to angle too much, simply unroll and re-roll. Try to minimize the unrolling/re-rolling as the wax can start to break apart.

12. Once you have finished rolling, gently press the edge of the wax into the candle. If the bottom isn't quite flat, you can press it into your cutting board to flatten it out.

13. Trim the wick if needed.
14. Repeat steps 8–13 for the remaining piece of wax.

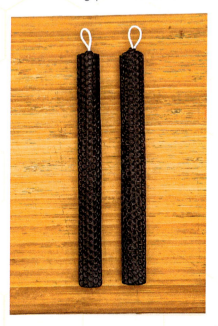

Spiral Tapers

With the spiral all the way down the candle, maintaining a tight roll as you go is the challenge here. These candles measure approximately 21 cm (8") tall and provide a unique look. These tapers are usually slightly larger than a standard taper holder, so you will likely have to compress the bottom of the candle to fit.

MATERIALS

- 1 – 21.5 x 41.5 cm (8.5 x 16") Sheet of beeswax in the color of your choice
- Wick (approximately 46 cm (18"))
- Sharp knife (I like to use an Exacto knife)
- Scissors
- Cutting board
- Ruler

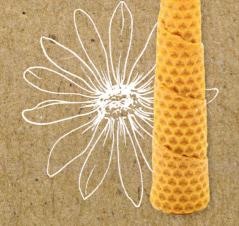

INSTRUCTIONS

1. If your sheet of wax has bloom on it or isn't very supple, gently heat it with a hair dryer. Be very careful not to melt it!

2. Place the beeswax sheet on the cutting board with the long edge facing you.

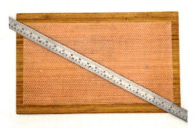

3. Cut the sheet in half diagonally.

4. If you want your candles to be the same height, stack the pieces of wax and trim any excess from the larger piece.

5. Set aside one of the pieces you just cut.

6. Cut a piece of wick the length of the short edge of one piece of wax plus a bit extra. I like to run the wick along the short edge of the wax so I can decide how much extra I would like to have coming out of the top.

7. Use the piece of wick you just cut as a template to cut another piece of wick. Set the extra wick aside.

8. Identify the V shape in the wick. The V will open to the top of your candle. This will help your candles burn better.

9. With the short edge of the wax facing you, align the wick along the edge of the wax, making sure the V shape of the wick is opening at the top of your candle, and the wick goes all the way to the bottom of the wax.

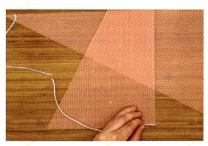

10. Gently roll the edge of the wax over the wick.

11. Roll the candle firmly, making sure the bottom stays flat. Keeping the candle tight and flat simultaneously is the challenge for this candle. If it starts to angle too much, simply unroll and re-roll. Try to minimize the unrolling/re-rolling as the wax can start to break apart.

12. Once you have finished rolling, gently press the edge of the wax into the candle. I like to press the wax in for at least one rotation around the candle to make sure it doesn't come apart. If the bottom isn't quite flat, you can press it into your cutting board to flatten it out.

13. Trim the wick if needed.
14. Repeat steps 8–13 for the remaining piece of wax.

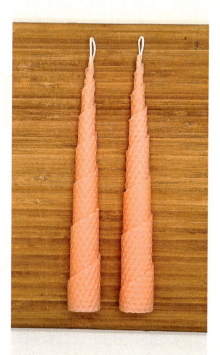

Pencil Tapers

It's very easy to customize this candle to your tastes. Simply change the angle of your cut to get different tapering effects. The height will vary based on the cut you choose, although the minimum height will be approximately just over 8" tall. These tapers will fit in a standard taper holder.

MATERIALS

- 1 – 21.5 x 41.5 cm (8.5 x 16") Sheet of beeswax in the color of your choice
- Wick (approximately 46 cm (18"))
- Sharp knife (I like to use an Exacto knife)
- Scissors
- Cutting board
- Ruler

INSTRUCTIONS

1. If your sheet of wax has bloom on it or isn't very supple, gently heat it with a hair dryer. Be very careful not to melt it!

2. Place the beeswax sheet on the cutting board with the long edge facing you.

3. Decide how much of a taper you would like on the top of the candle to determine your measurements. For example, if you would like 2.5 cm (1") of taper at the top, you will mark 21 cm (8.5") on the double hatch lines shown in the diagram. The single hatch lines will measure approximately 19 cm (7.5").

TIP: Sheet sizes vary, so I like to measure the length of the long edge and divide by two to find the midpoint. Add half the size of your desired taper size to the midpoint. Example: For a 41.5 cm (16") long sheet, the midpoint is 20 cm (8"). If I would like a 2.5 cm (1") taper, I will add 1.3 cm (0.5") to the midpoint to get the double hatch measurement of 21 cm (8.5").

> **SAMPLE CALCULATION**
>
> For a taper height of 0.5"
>
> length of double hatch lines = (width of sheet / 2) + (taper height / 2)
>
> length of double hatch lines = (16"/2) + (0.5"/2)
>
> length of double hatch lines = 8" + 0.25"
>
> length of double hatch lines = 8.25"
>
> length of single hatch lines = width of sheet − length of double hatch lines
>
> length of single hatch lines = 16" − 8.25"
>
> length of single hatch lines = 7.75"
>
> taper height = length of double hatch lines − length of single hatch lines
>
> taper height = 8.25" − 7.75"
>
> taper height = 0.5" − exactly what we desired!

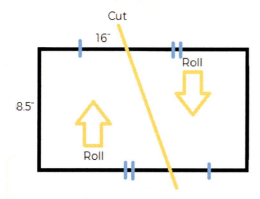

It also helps to mark each edge first, connect the markings with the ruler, and then cut.

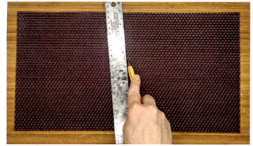

4. If you want your candles to be the same height, stack the pieces of wax and trim any excess from the larger piece.

5. Set aside one of the pieces you just cut.

6. Cut a piece of wick the length of the double-hatched edge of one piece of wax plus a bit extra. I like to run the wick along this edge so I can decide how much extra I would like to have coming out of the top.

7. Use the piece of wick you just cut as a template to cut another piece of wick. Set the extra wick aside.

8. Identify the V shape in the wick. The V will open to the top of your candle. This will help your candles burn better.

9. With the double-hatched edge of the wax facing you, align the wick along the edge of the wax, making sure the V shape of the wick is opening at the top of your candle, and the wick goes all the way to the bottom of the wax. The bottom of the candle will be the 21 cm (8.5") edge (originally the short edge of the sheet).

10. Gently roll the edge of the wax over the wick.

11. Roll the candle firmly, making sure the bottom stays flat. If it starts to angle too much, simply unroll and re-roll. Try to minimize the unrolling/re-rolling as the wax can start to break apart.

12. Once you have finished rolling, gently press the edge of the wax into the candle. If the bottom isn't quite flat, you can press it into your cutting board to flatten it out.

13. Trim the wick if needed.

14. Repeat steps 8-13 for the remaining piece of wax.

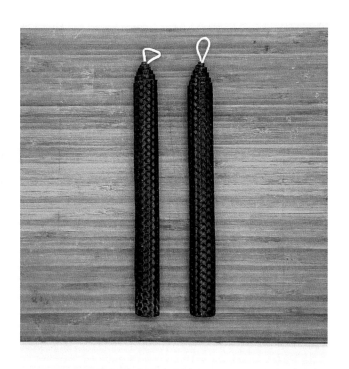

Fun Variations

- Once you have finished rolling your candle, instead of sealing the edge, unroll the outer layer. Use cookie cutters on your wax canvas to create fun designs.

- To eliminate wasted wax, make 2 candles in different colors and use the same cookie cutters on each candle. Swap the cutouts between the candles to make inverses!

- Make your own custom shapes by printing out simple graphics on paper. Cut these out and glue them on a piece of cardboard for stability if you plan on using them multiple times. Place the paper or cardboard on your wax canvas and cut out your custom shape.

- Instead of cutting shapes out of your candle with cookie cutters, try adding scraps of wax to the outside of your candle. Create wax flowers, a geometric pattern, or whatever your imagination can come up with!

Pillars

Add some sensuality to your space with pillars of all shapes and sizes. From the simple small pillar we'll make from one beeswax sheet here to taller and wider pillars, customize the size to suit your space.

Pillars are slightly more complex than tapers to make. For this candle, you will learn how to put together multiple pieces of wax.

SAFETY: Be very careful with knives. Always cut away from yourself and others. Keep your fingers out of the path of the knife!

TIPS AND TRICKS: Measure twice, cut once. If your taper is too big for its holder, gently mold the bottom of the candle until it fits.

Pillars are slightly more complex than tapers to make.

Simple Pillar

Grab a sheet of wax and get ready to make your very first pillar candle. These candles end up measuring approximately 10 cm (4") tall and 5 cm (2") wide.

MATERIALS

- 1 – 21.5 x 41.5 cm (8.5 x 16") Sheet of beeswax in the color of your choice
- Wick (approximately 11.5 cm (4.5"))
- Sharp knife (I like to use an Exacto knife)
- Scissors
- Cutting board
- Ruler

INSTRUCTIONS

1. If your sheet of wax has bloom on it or isn't very supple, gently heat it with a hair dryer. Be very careful not to melt it!

2. Place the beeswax sheet on the cutting board with a short edge facing you.

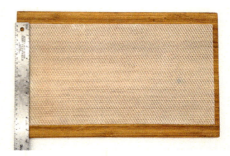

3. Mark the halfway point on the short edge.

4. Repeat the marking on the other short edge.

5. Connect the markings with the ruler and cut along the ruler.

6. If you want your candle to have a consistent height, stack the pieces of wax and trim any excess from the larger piece.

7. If you choose to have an inconsistent height in your candle, choose whether you would like a concave or convex candle. To make a concave candle, set aside the larger piece. For a convex candle, set aside the shorter piece.

8. Cut a piece of wick the length of the short edge of your piece of wax plus a bit extra. I like to run the wick along this edge so I can decide how much extra I would like to have coming out of the top.

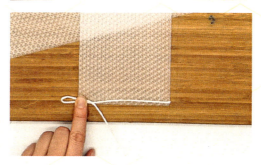

9. Identify the V shape in the wick. The V will open to the top of your candle. This will help your candles burn better.

10. With the short edge of the wax facing you, align the wick along the edge of the wax, making sure the V shape of the wick is opening at the top of your candle, and the wick goes all the way to the bottom of the wax.

11. Gently roll the edge of the wax over the wick.

12. Roll the candle firmly, making sure the bottom stays flat. If it starts to angle too much, simply unroll and re-roll. Try to minimize the unrolling/re-rolling as the wax can start to break apart.

13. Once you have finished rolling, grab your second piece of wax and line it up with the edge of the first.

I like to slightly overlap them to account for slippage.

14. Continue rolling the candle until the edge of the piece you have finished rolling is at the top. Don't worry about the bottom piece at this point other than making sure you are rolling along the edge of the second piece.

15. Bring the second piece of wax up to meet the end of the first piece and gently press the edges together. If the wax is overlapped too much or there is a gap between the pieces, adjust the first part of the candle until the wax meets. Watch the bottom stays even!

16. Continue rolling along the second piece until you reach the end.

17. Gently press the edge of the wax into the candle. If the bottom isn't quite flat, you can press it into your cutting board to flatten it out.

18. Trim the wick if needed.

Fun Variations
- Roll your candle in glitter to add some pizzazz.
- Use cookie cutters to cut shapes from different colors and add to your candles.
- Get a striped effect by rolling 2 colors of wax together in the spiral taper method. Just stack the two different colors of wax and follow the instructions above. Note that the base of these candles will be quite large and won't fit a standard taper holder.
- Flare your spiral tapers by gently pulling the edge of the wax away from the candle. This takes some practice!

Beehive

Inspired by the steps used in beekeeping thousands of years ago, these adorable candles use many pieces of wax to create. They are the most complex rolled candle we'll cover in this book.

SAFETY: Be very careful with knives. Always cut away from yourself and others. Keep your fingers out of the path of the knife!

TIPS AND TRICKS: Measure twice, cut once. Pay particular attention to the 2.5 cm (1") piece that ends at a point! Check the heights of matching pieces before rolling. Adjust mismatched pieces by trimming any excess before starting to roll. Burn your candle on a candle plate to catch any drips.

To make sure you don't measure from the wrong edge of the wax, move your ruler instead of the wax sheet.

Beehive

Read the instructions carefully! When complete, the beehive is approximately 3" tall.

MATERIALS

- 1 – 22 x 41.5 cm (8.5 x 16") Sheet of beeswax in the color of your choice
- Wick (approximately 11.5 cm (4.5"))
- Sharp knife (I like to use an Exacto knife)
- Scissors
- Cutting board
- Ruler

INSTRUCTIONS

1. If your sheet of wax has bloom on it or isn't very supple, gently heat it with a hair dryer. Be very careful not to melt it!

2. Place the beeswax sheet on the cutting board with a long edge facing you.

3. Mark the measurements shown in the following diagram:

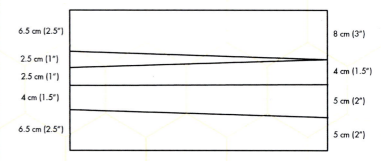

TIP: To make sure you don't measure from the wrong edge of the wax, move your ruler instead of the wax sheet.

4. Connect the markings with the ruler and cut along the ruler. Pay particular attention to the 2.5 cm (1") piece that ends at a point!

5. Lay all the pieces out to make one large triangle. Match the edges with the same measurements (6.5 cm (2.5") to 6.5 cm (2.5"), 5 cm (2") to 5 cm (2"), 4 cm (1.5") to 4 cm (1.5"), and 2.5 cm (1") to 2.5 cm (1")).

6. Check the heights at each of the connections to make sure they match. If there is a difference, trim the excess.

7. Cut a piece of wick to fit the tallest piece of wax plus a bit extra (this wax piece should be approximately 8 cm (3"). I like to run the wick along this edge so I can decide how much extra I would like to have coming out of the top.

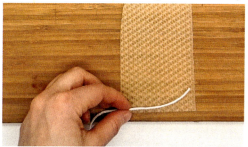

8. Identify the V shape in the wick. The V will open to the top of your candle. This will help your candles burn better.

9. With the short edge of the largest piece of wax facing you, align the wick along the edge of the wax, making sure the V shape of the wick is opening at the top of your candle, and the wick goes all the way to the bottom of the wax.

10. Gently roll the edge of the wax over the wick.

11. Roll the candle firmly, making sure the bottom stays flat. If it starts to angle too much, simply unroll and re-roll. Try to minimize the unrolling/re-rolling as the wax can start to break apart.

12. At the end of your piece, grab the next largest piece of wax and line it up with the edge of the first. I like to slightly overlap them to account for slippage.

13. Continue rolling the candle until the edge of the piece you have finished rolling is at the top. Don't worry about the bottom piece at this point other than making sure you are rolling along the edge of the second piece.

14. Bring the new piece of wax up to meet the end of the already rolled piece and gently press the edges together. If the wax is overlapped too much or there is a gap between the pieces, adjust the first part of the candle until the wax meets. Make sure the bottom stays even!

15. Continue rolling along this piece until you reach the end, making sure it is tight, and the bottom is flat.

16. Repeat steps 12–15 with the remaining pieces of wax.

17. Gently press the edge of the wax into the candle. I like to press in the edge all along the bottom of the candle at least once to make sure it stays. If the bottom isn't quite flat, you can press it into your cutting board to flatten it out.

18. Trim the wick if needed.

Fun Variations

- Leave extra wick at the top of your candle to add interest.
- Try tying a tag to the excess wick.
- Roll the candle in fine glitter for extra pizzazz.
- Add a small bee pin or magnet to the outside of the candle. Once the candle has been burned, it can be reused. A ladybug would be cute too!

These are just a few ideas to get you started. The possibilities are endless!

Dipped Candles

The key here is to find a melting vat deep enough to get the desired candle height.

CHAPTER 11
Dipped Candles

Dipped candles are a ton of fun to make for all ages! I remember making my first dipped candle at a summer camp one year when I was visiting my cousin. The candles turned out a little bit lumpy, but they were super fun to make! In this chapter we'll take a look at some different setups for making dipped candles as well as some project ideas for special occasions and every day.

MATERIALS

It's very easy to get started making dipped candles. With a few supplies, you'll be off to the races in no time!

- 1 – Double boiler setup (see Chapter 6 for instructions) — getting the right melting vat is important
- Beeswax
- Wick (see Chapter 2 for more information)
- Binder clips (see below)
- Weight (one per candle)
- Scissors
- Knife (optional)
- Chopsticks or dowels (optional)
- Aluminum foil (optional)
- Thermometer (optional)

Melting Vat

The key here is to find a melting vat deep enough to get the desired candle height. When I choose a melting vat, I look for a container that is tall and narrow to be most efficient with the wax. When I was first starting, I found this stainless-steel pot at a second-hand store that worked perfectly for making 20–23 cm (8–9") tall tapers.

Binder Clips

Binder clips are also my best friend for dipped tapers. I'm able to make two standard-sized taper candles with a 1 ¼" binder clip. The setup is sometimes a bit tricky, but I find them easy to hang onto for dipping, and it's easy to dip multiples at the beginning using a chopstick, skewer, or dowel if the melting vat is wide enough.

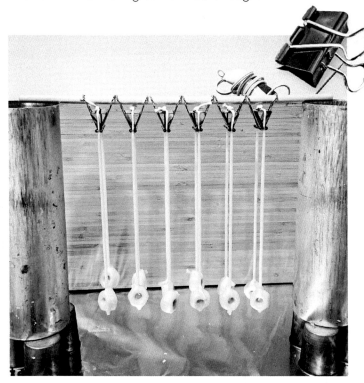

Weight

Finally, a weight rounds out the list of helpful materials. The weight will keep the wick taut and help you keep track of the bottom of your candle. I like using stainless steel nuts—they are easy to find and inexpensive at your local hardware store (also see the note on stainless steel in Chapter 1).

TIPS: Your candles will need to cool a bit between dips. It's handy to make a bunch at once, so having a place to hang them is extremely helpful. I like to use a few chopsticks or dowels at the edge of the counter near the melting vat. Make sure the ends of your hanging device on the counter are weighted down enough so your candles don't end up on the floor!

Drips are common, so it's helpful to protect the surface around your dipping station with aluminum foil. I put some down under the hanging device to catch any drips from freshly dipped candles. When you're finished for the day, put the foil in the freezer. Once the drips have cooled, they are easy to remove and re-melt.

Practice makes perfect, and taper candles are easy to re-start if you don't like your results. Simply hold your dipped candle in the hot wax until the wax re-melts. Let your wick cool down a bit, and you're ready to go again!

SAFETY: Be very careful of hot wax (especially drips after a dip!) and steam. Try to minimize the distance between your double boiler and cooling station. Make sure your path is clear before moving your freshly dipped candles to the cooling station. If you burn yourself, take appropriate first aid actions. Please review the safety precautions in Chapter 9 before working through this chapter.

Dipped Candles

Once your wax is set up and you have created a cooling station (if you decide to make many candles at once), it's time to prepare your wick and get ready to dip! Regardless of the size of candle, your setup steps will be very similar.

1. Set up your double boiler with the beeswax on the stove on low-medium heat.
2. Lay out your aluminum foil. (Optional)
3. Prepare the wick. Cut the wick to the height of your choice. When you measure, be sure to account for tying the weight and have enough space at the top to clip with the binder clip (this will be the end you light as well).

4. Tie your weight to the bottom of the wick and clip the top of the wick to the binder clip (see below for specific instructions for different types of candles).

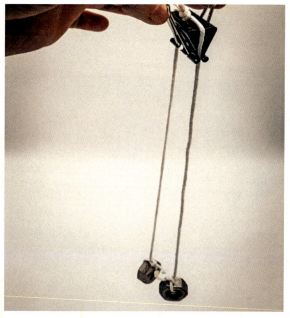

5. If needed, stir unmelted wax into the melted wax (this is usually only necessary if a piece of wax is stuck to the side of the melting vat or if you are re-melting wax that was already in the melting vat).

6. If you are using a thermometer, check the temperature of the wax. As a reminder, the optimal pouring temperature for beeswax is 61–66°C (142–151°F).

7. If you are not using a thermometer, the wax should be melted but not too hot. A quick test you can do is to dip a skewer or chopstick into the wax. The wax should form a thin, smooth layer. If the wax is too hot, the layer will be very thin and perhaps patchy (more wax on the part closer to your fingers that spent less time in the wax). If the wax is too cool, ridges may form on the wax layer (although this can also be caused by unsteady dipping as well). It takes a bit of practice, so experiment away! Dipped candles are very easy to redo, so don't worry if you don't get it right the first few times.

8. Prime the wick. The first time you dip the wick into the wax, allow the wick to absorb wax. This is called priming the wick. While you are holding the wick in the wax, watch for tiny air bubbles coming to the surface. When the air bubbles stop, your wick is primed and ready to go. It can be removed from the wax and cooled before you start dipping again.

9. Straighten the wick. If the wick isn't quite straight, gently straighten it. This usually happens if the weights stick together when dipping. It's important to keep it straight at the beginning. As the layers build, any deviations will become apparent. It's fairly easy to straighten within the first few layers, so don't worry too much if you don't get it quite straight the first dip.

10. Dip the candle. To prevent uneven wax distribution, keep your motion steady. As soon as you've submerged the candle fully, steadily pull it straight up. If you dip too quickly, your candles may start to swing and end up sticking to each other (this leaves imperfections on the candle). If you dip too slowly, the wax on your wick will start to re-melt. Experiment until you find the perfect dipping speed for you!

11. Catch the drips! Before moving the candle into your cooling station, gently drag the bottom of the weight against your melting vat to catch any drips.

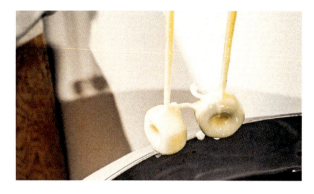

12. Allow the candle to cool. Between dips, it's important to give your candle a bit of time to solidify. This will help reduce the amount of wax that melts on your next dip. Making four sets at a time gives the candles plenty of time to cool between dips (they will still be warm for your next dip, especially as the size of your candle builds).

13. Trim off weights. Once your candle starts to build up enough size to prevent bending 0.5 cm (.25" or so in diameter), the weights can be trimmed off.

Cut off the weights with scissors or a sharp knife. The bottom of the candle may distort at this step, but the warm wax will allow you to mold it back into shape. Once you're happy with the shape, continue dipping.

14. When the candle is almost the correct size for your project (if I'm using a holder, I will check the size against the holder), make sure the bottom looks tidy. I like to cut off any excess drips I've missed and even out the bottom two to three dips before the candle is the correct size. Once you're happy with the bottom, complete your last dips and make sure you have a perfect fit!

15. Unclip the tops of the wicks, trim any stray drip marks from the bottom (be careful not to catch your cutting tool on the bottom of your wick this time!), and you're done!

Birthday Candles

Recommended wick starting point: #3/0 cotton square braid (see Chapter 2; test, test, test!)

These tiny treasures are quick and easy dips to make. I usually make these individually and clip four wicks with one 3 cm (1.25") binder clip. Since these are so small, I tend to skip the weights and manually straighten the candles instead. When I'm at the last few dips, I'll remove all the candles from the binder clip and dip them individually to make sure they are all about the same size.

Standard Tapers

Recommended wick starting point: #3/0 cotton square braid (see Chapter 2; test, test, test!)

I like to make my tapers in pairs. When cutting the wick, I add extra at the top and bottom to allow for the dipping apparatus (such as a binder clip) and the weights. Once the wicks are cut, add weights to the bottom of each length of wick. After that, I'll look for similarly sized wicks with weights and tie them in an overhand knot at the top.

When I am clipping the candles with the binder clip, I make sure the knot is in the middle, run the wick to the edges, and clip the wick as close to the edges as I can. Gently pull on the wick to simulate the weight of the candle as its dipped to make sure the wick doesn't slip out (if it does while you are dipping, you can always let the candle cool a bit and reset the clip).

At the step where the weight is removed, I shift the knotted end of the wick to the inside of the binder clip (pictured below). I tend to dip close to the edge of the binder clip, so this helps me to create a clean, well-formed top to the candle.

When reaching the final few dips, I'll remove the set from the binder clip entirely and test each candle in the holder (they sometimes fit a bit differently). From here, I dip each candle individually until the desired size is reached.

Things to Watch For

Drips—keep an eye out for stray drips when you're moving your candle from the melting vat to the cooling station. I've dripped wax on clothing, the floor, and skin at this stage many times!

Adding unmelted wax—as your wax level gets lower, you may need to add additional wax to have enough room to dip your candles. Make sure the wax is completely melted before continuing to dip (or it is at least out of the path of your dip if you're impatient like me!). If you catch your candle on the edge of the melting wax as you dip, it can create divets in the candles or stick them together. Depending on the depth I'm working with, I'll use a skewer or chopstick to check the depth of the wax I have to work with. This also works well when you are re-melting wax left in the melting vat from a previous candle-making session.

Fun Variations

Beeswax is malleable, which gives you a ton of options for creating fun shapes! Here are a few ideas to get you started:

- Zig zag
- Spiral
- Letters and numbers

You can also add decorative touches to the outer layer of the candle. Before you dip the candle for the last time, place your decoration on the candle. Dip the candle one last time to seal it. Pressed leaves or flowers work as great options (make sure you test for flammability!).

83

Poured Candles

Tips: Protect your pouring surface with aluminum foil. This will catch any drips and keep your space wax free. Once the candles have set, remove them and put the foil in the freezer. Once the drips have cooled, they are easy to remove and re-melt.

CHAPTER 12
Poured Beeswax Candles

Poured candles are fairly simple to create, although there is a risk of burning yourself with hot wax and possibly steam burns, depending on the double boiler method you use. Keep an eye on the temperature of your wax to prevent cracking. In this chapter, we will look at different types of poured beeswax candles along with ideas for variations to add some pizzazz to your designs.

Tealights

I love tealights! Whether it's a candlelit bath or just in the living room on cold and dark winter evenings, they are practical, functional, and easy to put nearly anywhere. It's so easy to change your décor with a simple candle holder or add some additional scent to a room with an oil burner or melter.

TIPS: Protect your pouring surface with aluminum foil. This will catch any drips and keep your space wax free. Once the candles have set, remove them and put the foil in the freezer. Once the drips have cooled, they are easy to remove and re-melt.

SAFETY: Be very careful of hot wax and steam. Try to minimize the distance between your double boiler and pouring space. Make sure your path is clear before transporting hot wax to the pouring station. If you burn yourself, take appropriate first aid actions. Please review the safety precautions in Chapter 9 before working through this section.

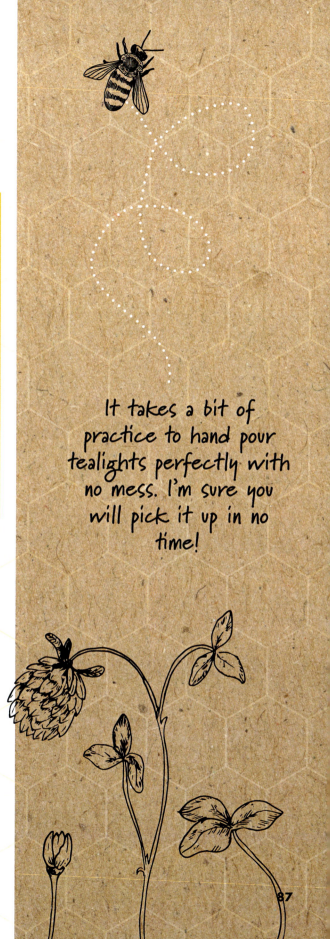

It takes a bit of practice to hand pour tealights perfectly with no mess. I'm sure you will pick it up in no time!

Simple Tealight

Tealights are one of my favourite types of candles because they are so versatile! Since tealight cups tend to be quite small, it takes a bit of practice to pour without overflow. Practice makes perfect!

MATERIALS:

- 1 – Double boiler (see Chapter 6 for instructions)
- Beeswax
- Suggested wick size as a starting point - Pre-tabbed wicks (try HTP104-25 to start)
- Tealight cups (polycarbonate or metal)
- Stirring utensil (optional; skewers and chopsticks work great)
- Aluminum foil (optional)
- Thermometer (optional)

INSTRUCTIONS:

1. Set up your double boiler with the beeswax on the stove on low-medium heat.
2. Lay out your aluminum foil. (Optional)
3. Place the tealight cups on your workspace. This will be on the foil if you have chosen to use it. If you are making more than one tealight, make sure the tealight cups are not touching. If they are and you pour them a bit too full, the meniscus may break causing the wax to spill over the edge.

4. When the wax has melted, dip the bottom of a pre-tabbed wick in the wax.

5. Center the tab in a tealight cup and press down firmly.

6. Let it cool for a minute and then straighten the wick.

7. Repeat steps 4-6 for all of the tealights you plan to make. Make sure there is still some space between the tealights.

8. If needed, stir unmelted wax into the melted wax (this is usually only necessary if a piece of wax is stuck to the side of the melting vat or if you are re-melting wax that was already in the melting vat).

9. If you are using a thermometer, check the temperature of the wax before pouring. As a reminder, the optimal pouring temperature for beeswax is 61–66°C (142–151°F).

If you are not using a thermometer, the wax should be melted but not too hot. To test this, pour a small amount of wax to just cover the bottom of a tealight cup.

Observe how long it takes to solidify on the bottom. At the ideal pouring temperature, it should stay liquid while you pour and solidify just on the bottom and sides soon after the pouring stops. If a film develops on the top right away, the wax isn't quite warm enough. If the edges of the tealight cup stay liquid for more than 45–60 seconds, the wax is too hot.

Another test I sometimes use is a 'pretend pour' where I am pouring the wax out of the melting vat so it just travels up the side of the melting vat. If the wax pours easily and leaves a small layer of cooled wax when the vat is righted, the temperature is okay.

If the wax resists pouring, the wax is too cool. If the wax pours easily and doesn't leave a small layer of wax, the wax is too hot. It takes a bit of practice to know when the right pouring conditions exist without a thermometer.

10. Once your wax is at the correct pouring temperature, carefully pour the wax into the prepared tealight cups until a slight meniscus forms.

Things to Watch For

Cracking—if the pouring temperature is too hot or the tealight cup isn't filled completely, your tealights may crack. See Chapter 14 for strategies to fix this.

Overflow—if your tealights overflow, allow them to solidify and then remove them from your workspace while they are still warm. Use a paper towel or rag to gently remove any drips while the candle is still warm. Be gentle during this process as squeezing may cause some cracking.

Since tealight cups tend to be quite small, it takes a bit of practice to pour without overflow. Practice makes perfect!

Votives

Votives

A votive is "an object placed in a sacred location in honour of a god, goddess, or saint, typically as an expression of thanks in fulfilment of a vow." The word is derived from the 16th century Latin votivus, which meant "expressing a desire." Today, votives are still used in Christian denominations for prayer intentions. Most votives are designed to be burned in a container slightly larger than the candle itself called a votive holder. These can range from a simple glass holder you pick up from a dollar store to more elaborate etched or decorated holders.

TIPS: Protect your pouring surface with aluminum foil. This will catch any drips and keep your space wax free. Once the candles have set, remove them and put the foil in the freezer. Once the drips have cooled, they are easy to remove and re-melt.

I find removing votives from the mold when solidified but still warm makes removing wick pins easier. As soon as the wax has cooled enough to pull away from the sides of the mold, I gently remove the candle. If it doesn't come out right away, allow it to cool for a bit longer. The candle should still feel warm to the touch after it has been removed, and metal molds will still be warm as well. From here, place the tip of the wick pin on your workspace and gently press down. The wax should be warm enough at the center of the candle for the pin to be easily removed. If you remove the pin too early, liquid wax may spill into the wick space. Grab a wick and try to put it into the candle. If it doesn't go in easily, throw the candle back into the melting pot and start again. Most of the time, the wax will be warm enough for wicking to be no problem!

SAFETY: Be very careful of hot wax and steam. Try to minimize the distance between your double boiler and pouring space. Make sure your path is clear before transporting hot wax to the pouring station. If you burn yourself, take appropriate first aid actions. Please review the safety precautions in Chapter 9 before working through this section.

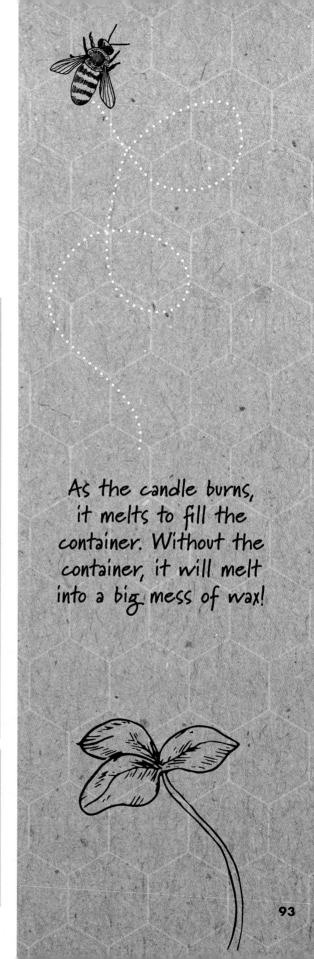

As the candle burns, it melts to fill the container. Without the container, it will melt into a big mess of wax!

Simple Votive

For these candles, you will need a mold and optionally a wick pin. It's important to pour until you can see the meniscus above the mold to make it easier to remove and prevent cracking.

MATERIALS

- 1 – Double boiler setup (see Chapter 6 for instructions)
- Beeswax
- Pre-tabbed wicks or a wick pin
- Votive mold (metal or silicone)
- Stirring utensil (optional; skewers and chopsticks work great)
- Aluminum foil (optional)
- Thermometer (optional)

INSTRUCTIONS:

1. Set up your double boiler with the beeswax on the stove on low-medium heat.

2. Lay out your aluminum foil. (Optional)

3. Place the votive molds on your workspace. This will be on the foil if you have chosen to use it. If you are making more than one votive, make sure the molds are not touching. If they are touching and you pour to the meniscus, the wax will spill over the edge. If you are using a wick pin, place your wick pin in the mold and center. Skip to step 5 when you are finished. If you are using a wick, continue to step 4.

4. When the wax has melted, dip the bottom of a pre-tabbed wick in the wax (if you are using a wick). Center the tab in the votive mold and press down firmly. Let it cool for a minute and then straighten the wick. Repeat this step for all the votives you plan to make. Make sure there is still some space between the molds.

5. If needed, stir unmelted wax into the melted wax (this is usually only necessary if a piece of wax is stuck to the side of the melting vat or if you are re-melting wax that was already in the melting vat).

6. If you are using a thermometer, check the temperature of the wax before pouring. As a reminder, the optimal pouring temperature for beeswax is 61–66°C (142–151°F).

7. If you are not using a thermometer, the wax should be melted but not too hot. To test this, pour a small amount of wax to just cover the bottom of votive mold. Observe how long it takes to solidify on the bottom. At the ideal pouring temperature, it should stay liquid while you pour and solidify just on the bottom and sides soon after the pouring stops. If a film develops on the top right away, the wax isn't quite warm enough. If the edges of the mold stay liquid for more than 10–15 seconds, the wax is too hot. Another test I sometimes use is a 'pretend pour'

where I am pouring the wax out of the melting vat so it just travels up the side of the melting vat. If the wax pours easily and doesn't leave a small layer of wax, the wax is too hot. It takes a bit of practice to know when the right pouring conditions exist without a thermometer.

8. Once your wax is at the correct pouring temperature, carefully pour the wax into the prepared molds until a slight meniscus forms. If you are using wick pins, skip to step 10.

9. When are you are done pouring, straighten any wicks if necessary.
10. Allow your votives to cool.
11. Once your votives have cooled, they will pull away from the edges of your mold. This will make it easy for you to remove them.

If needed, gently wiggle the candle back and forth until it releases from the mold.

If you are still having trouble removing the candle from the mold, place it in the freezer for half an hour or so. If this doesn't work and you are using a metal mold, gently apply heat to the mold until the candle releases.

12. If you used a wick pin, carefully remove it If the pin doesn't move with gentle pressure, I gently tap the pin with a hammer until it releases.
13. If you used a wick pin, thread a pre-tabbed wick through the hole left by the pin.

Things to Watch For

Cracking—with votives, cracking tends to happen if you don't pour enough wax into the mold. When I have cracked votives, I've found redoing them is the easiest way to go.

Overflow—if your votives overflow, allow them to solidify and then remove them from your workspace while they are still warm. Use a paper towel or rag to gently remove any drips while the candle is still warm. Be gentle during this process as squeezing may cause cracking.

Stuck wick pin—if your wick pin is stuck, I use a rubber mallet or hammer to gently tap the top of the wick pin. Be aware of how much force you are using as you can damage the wick pin. If you prefer, use heat to gently heat the wick pin, being careful not to melt the candle. As the metal warms, it should slip out of the candle.

Pillars

Candles were originally used to provide light and for religious purposes. Today, however, we are able to find candles in all shapes, sizes, colors, and scents. Pillars are no different. In this section, we'll first explore making a straight pillar (meaning a cylindrical or rectangular prism shaped candle with the same diameter along the height of the candle) and then move on to fun shapes and sizes.

TIPS: Protect your pouring surface with aluminum foil. This will catch any drips and keep your space wax free. Once the candles have set, remove them and put the foil in the freezer. Once the drips have cooled, they are easy to remove and re-melt.

SAFETY: Be very careful of hot wax and steam. Try to minimize the distance between your double boiler and pouring space. Make sure your path is clear before transporting hot wax to the pouring station. If you burn yourself, take appropriate first aid actions. Please review the safety precautions in Chapter 9 before working through this section.

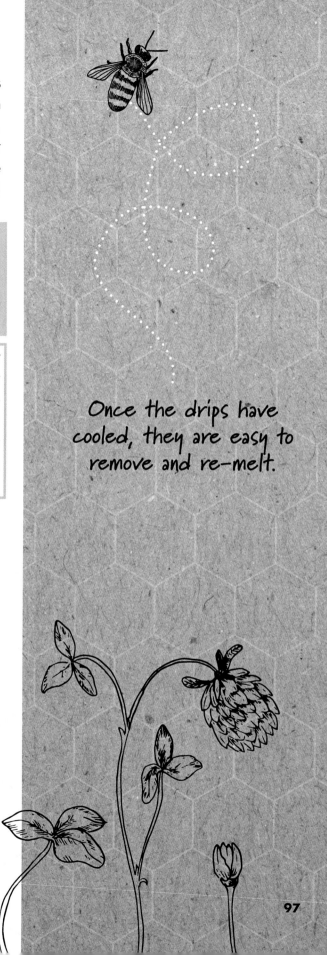

Once the drips have cooled, they are easy to remove and re-melt.

Simple Pillar

Pillar molds are available in metal, silicone, and plastic. I use metal molds and will share my process with you here.

MATERIALS:

- 1 – Double boiler setup (see Chapter 6 for instructions)
- Beeswax
- Wick (varies based on the mold you are using)
- Mold (metal, silicone, or plastic)
- Rubber plug
- Wick centering tool (if you don't have one, skewers, chopsticks, and pencils work great)
- Stand (used tealight cups or small blocks of wood of the same size work well. Whatever you choose to use, make sure they are the same height and will stand up to the weight of the wax you are pouring!)
- Stirring utensil (optional; skewers and chopsticks work great)
- Aluminum foil (optional)
- Thermometer (optional)

INSTRUCTIONS:

1. Set up your double boiler with the beeswax on the stove on low-medium heat.
2. Lay out your aluminum foil. (Optional)
3. Prepare your mold. Thread the mold with wick, making sure the wick braid is in the correct direction for the top of your candle.

4. Tie the wick to your wick centering tool at the open part of your mould.

5. Make sure the wick is centered and pulled taut before using your rubber plug to plug the wick hole.

6. Set up your stand on the foil if you have chosen to use it. Place the mold on your stand. I make mine out of a couple of tealight cups since they are usually handy.

The rubber plug protrudes from the bottom of the mold, so work around the plug to make sure the mold is level.

7. Once your mold is stable and level, adjust the wick so it is centered in the mold. Pay attention to where your wick centering tool is located and plan where you will pour the wax. If you need to adjust the location of the tool or the mold, do so now.

8. If needed, stir unmelted wax into the melted wax (this is usually only necessary if a piece of wax is stuck to the side of the melting vat or if you are re-melting wax that was already in the melting vat).

9. If you are using a thermometer, check the temperature of the wax before pouring. As a reminder, the optimal pouring temperature for beeswax is 61–66°C (142–151°F).

10. If you are not using a thermometer, the wax should be melted but not too hot. To test this, pour a small amount of wax to just cover the bottom of the mold. Observe how long it takes to solidify on the bottom. At the ideal pouring temperature, it should stay liquid while you pour and solidify just on the bottom soon after the pouring stops. If a film develops on the top right away, the wax isn't quite warm enough. If wax runs out of the bottom of the mold or you can see the bottom of the mold for more than 10–15 seconds, the wax is too hot. Another test I sometimes use is a 'pretend pour' where I am pouring the wax out of the melting vat so it just travels up the side of the melting vat. If the wax pours easily and leaves a small layer of cooled wax when the vat is righted, the temperature is okay. If the wax resists pouring, the wax is too cool. If the wax pours easily and doesn't leave a small layer of wax, the wax is too hot. It takes a bit of practice to know when the right pouring conditions exist without a thermometer.

11. Once your wax is at the correct pouring temperature, carefully pour the wax into the prepared mold. Sometimes my plug isn't quite perfect and there are some drips out of the bottom of the mold, so I tend to start with a very small amount of wax to start. As I continue adding wax, I try to make sure the area around the plug remains solid to be extra safe. This could mean doing a handful or more pours to complete the candle. The key here is to do your subsequent pours before the candle starts to cool enough to release from the sides of the mold. If the top level solidifies (perhaps you have forgotten about your candle like I do sometimes!), I like to poke holes in the candle with a skewer or chopstick to help the different layers of wax adhere to each other.

12. Allow your candle to cool.

13. Once your pillar has cooled, it will pull away from the edges of your mold. This will make it easy for you to remove. If the wax is stuck to the sides and you are using a metal mold, you may need to gently apply heat to the mold until the candle releases. If the candle only appears to be stuck in one area, putting your mold in the freezer for a few hours or firmly tapping the opposite side of the mold with the heel of your hand may help it release.

14. After you have removed your candle from the mold, cut the wick as close to the bottom of the candle as possible. I like to do this when the candle is still slightly warm if possible so it's easy to repair any nicks. After trimming the wick, you can smooth out the bottom with a heat gun.

15. Finally, trim the wick to the desired size at the top of the candle. I like to leave at least 1 cm (0.5") of wick.

Protect your pouring surface with aluminum foil.

Things to Watch For

Cracking—if your wax is too hot, you will end up with a cracked candle. Sometimes pouring multiple times can help with this if you allow the wax to cool before each subsequent pour.

Wax comes out the bottom—if you find the wax is coming out the bottom of your candle, allow the bottom to cool a bit before continuing your pour. I like to pour a small amount of wax into the mold and that the bottom of the mold is no longer visible. From here, add a bit more hot wax and make sure the bottom of the mold is still covered in cooling wax.

If you notice the bottom layer begin to show through to the mold, let the wax cool slightly before adding more.

Wax pulls away from the edges—this is normal behavior for beeswax.

Containers

Containers

It's very important to test your containers thoroughly and safely in case the heat of the wax affects the container. Teacups, for example, are designed to withstand hot beverages normally served between 71.1°C (160°F) and 85°C (185°F). Since beeswax melts at 61–66°C (142–151°F), this would be a good container choice. Get creative in your container choices and remember to test them safely and carefully before using every day or giving them away.

TIPS: Protect your pouring surface with aluminum foil. This will catch any drips and keep your space wax free. Once the candles have set, remove them and put the foil in the freezer. Once the drips have cooled, they are easy to remove and re-melt.

When burn testing a new container, isolate it somewhere where if breakage occurs, you can minimize the mess and risk of fire. The kitchen sink is perfect for this! However, it is advisable to cover your drain to prevent wax from clogging it. A bit of aluminum foil folded up in a bowl shape is extremely useful. It can also help to check your potential containers for any chips or cracks that could cause breakage.

SAFETY: Be very careful of hot wax and steam. Try to minimize the distance between your double boiler and pouring space. Make sure your path is clear before transporting hot wax to the pouring station. If you burn yourself, take appropriate first aid actions. Please review the safety precautions in Chapter 9 before working through this section.

Get creative in your container choices and remember to test them safely and carefully before using every day or giving them away.

Mason Jar Candle

Mason jars make great container candles! In canning, it is recommended to simmer jars to 82°C (180°F) prior to putting food in them, which is well above the temperature at which beeswax melts. They are a great option for rustic décor and can easily be decorated and customized to fit specific themes or weddings.

MATERIALS:

- 1 – Double boiler setup (see Chapter 6 for instructions)
- Beeswax
- Pre-tabbed wicks (try HTP1212-65 to start)
- Mason jar
- Wick centering tool (optional; if you don't have one, eyeball the center)
- Stirring utensil (optional; skewers and chopsticks work great)
- Aluminum foil (optional)
- Thermometer (optional)

INSTRUCTIONS:

1. Set up your double boiler with the beeswax on the stove on low-medium heat.
2. Lay out your aluminum foil. (Optional)
3. Place the mason jar(s) on your workspace. This will be on the foil if you have chosen to use it.

4. When the wax has melted, dip the bottom of a pre-tabbed wick in the wax. Center the tab in a tealight cup and press down firmly. Let it cool for a minute and then straighten the wick. Repeat this step for all the mason jars you plan to make.

5. If needed, stir unmelted wax into the melted wax (this is usually only necessary if a piece of wax is stuck to the side of the melting vat or if you are re-melting wax that was already in the melting vat).
6. If you are using a thermometer, check the temperature of the wax before pouring. As a reminder, the optimal pouring temperature for beeswax is 61–66°C (142–151°F).
7. If you are not using a thermometer, the wax should be melted but not too hot. To test this, pour a small amount of wax to just cover the bottom of the jar. Observe how long it takes to solidify on the bottom. At the ideal pouring temperature, it should stay liquid while you pour and solidify just on the bottom and sides soon after the

pouring stops. If a film develops on the top right away, the wax isn't quite warm enough. If the edges stay liquid for more than 10–15 seconds, the wax is too hot. Another test I sometimes use is a 'pretend pour' where I am pouring the wax out of the melting vat so it just travels up the side of the melting vat. If the wax pours easily and leaves a small layer of cooled wax when the vat is righted, the temperature is okay. If the wax resists pouring, the wax is too cool. If the wax pours easily and doesn't leave a small layer of wax, the wax is too hot. It takes a bit of practice to know when the right pouring conditions exist without a thermometer.

8. Once your wax is at the correct pouring temperature, carefully pour a small amount of wax into the prepared mason jar until the wick tab is completely under the wax. Allow the wax to solidify (it should only take a minute or two until it solidifies) and straighten the wick.

9. Poke holes into the cooled wax to improve adherence between layers. Pour wax into the jar until it is approximately 2/3 of the way to the amount you would like filled with wax. Once you have a feel for the correct pouring temperature, you can do a full pour.

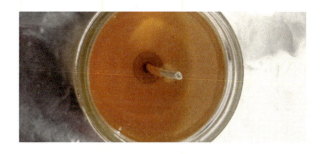

10. When are you are done pouring, straighten any wicks if necessary.

11. Allow the wax to cool.

Things to Watch For

Cracking—if your wax is too hot, you will end up with a cracked candle. You can pre-empt this by pouring twice (once to 2/3 full and once to top it off) until you get the hang of it.

Wax pulls away from the edges—this is normal behavior for beeswax. If you would prefer the wax to go right to the edges of the container, you can gently heat the container until the wax starts to liquefy again. With mason jars, you can see how the wax looks through the sides of the glass. It might take a few tries until you are happy with how the candles look through the jar and to get the wax all the way to the edge.

Teacup Candle

Teacup candles are absolutely adorable! They make fantastic gifts and are a great way to bring any heirloom teacups you have out of storage and into use. Hot beverages are often served between 71.1°C (160°F) and 85°C (185°F), and teacups must withstand these temperatures. Teacup candles are great for everyday décor, gifts, and wedding favors.

MATERIALS:

- 1 – Double boiler setup (see Chapter 6 for instructions)
- Beeswax
- Pre-tabbed wicks (try HTP1212-65 to start)
- Teacup
- Wick centering tool (optional; if you don't have one, eyeball the center)
- Stirring utensil (optional; skewers and chopsticks work great)
- Aluminum foil (optional)
- Thermometer (optional)

INSTRUCTIONS:

1. Set up your double boiler with the beeswax on the stove on low-medium heat.
2. Lay out your aluminum foil. (Optional)
3. Place the teacup(s) on your workspace. This will be on the foil if you have chosen to use it.

4. When the wax has melted, dip the bottom of a pre-tabbed wick in the wax. Center the tab in a tealight cup and press down firmly. Let it cool for a minute and then straighten the wick. Repeat this step for all the teacups you plan to make.

5. If needed, stir unmelted wax into the melted wax (this is usually only necessary if a piece of wax is stuck to the side of the melting vat or if you are re-melting wax that was already in the melting vat).
6. If you are using a thermometer, check the temperature of the wax before pouring. As a reminder, the optimal pouring temperature for beeswax is 61–66°C (142–151°F).
7. If you are not using a thermometer, the wax should be melted but not too hot. To test this, pour a small amount of wax to just cover the bottom of the teacup. Observe how long it takes to solidify on the bottom. At the

ideal pouring temperature, it should stay liquid while you pour and solidify just on the bottom and sides soon after the pouring stops. If a film develops on the top right away, the wax isn't quite warm enough. If the edges of the teacup cup stay liquid for more than 10–15 seconds, the wax is too hot. Another test I sometimes use is a 'pretend pour' where I am pouring the wax out of the melting vat so it just travels up the side of the melting vat. If the wax pours easily and leaves a small layer of cooled wax when the vat is righted, the temperature is okay. If the wax resists pouring, the wax is too cool. If the wax pours easily and doesn't leave a small layer of wax, the wax is too hot. It takes a bit of practice to know when the right pouring conditions exist without a thermometer.

8. Once your wax is at the correct pouring temperature, carefully pour a small amount of wax into the prepared teacup until the wick tab is completely under the wax. Allow the wax to solidify (it should only take a minute or two until it solidifies) and straighten the wick.

9. Poke holes into the cooled wax to improve adherence between layers. Pour wax into the jar until it is approximately 2/3 of the way to the amount you would like filled with wax. Once you have a feel for the correct pouring temperature, you can do a full pour.

10. When are you are done pouring, straighten any wicks if necessary.

11. Allow the wax to cool.

Things to Watch For

Cracking—if your wax is too hot, you will end up with a cracked candle. You can pre-empt this by pouring twice (once to 2/3 full and once to top it off) until you get the hang of it.

Wax pulls away from the edges—this is normal behavior for beeswax. If you would prefer the wax to go right to the edges of the container, you can gently heat the top of the candle until the wax liquefies and spills into the spaces. It might take a few tries until you are happy with how the candle looks. By heating the wax from above, you will likely melt some of the wax coating on your pre-tabbed wick, causing it to fray. You can leave it, press it together to fix it, or trim the wick before giving your candle. I find the wick doesn't look as nice after reheating the wax.

Wick size—teacups come in all shapes and sizes, so it's important to test your wicks! What works well for one teacup may not work as well for another. I wick similarly sized teacups the same and change my wicks when the size difference is significant.

Fun Variations

Once you've made your first few container candles, I'm sure you will be hooked! Here are a few ideas of other containers you might use:

- Old glass candle jars
- Coffee cups
- Vintage vessels (find these at thrift stores, garage sales, estate sales, and more!)

Adding Dye

I have a lot of fun mixing new colors. A brand new recipe can be a bit of a pain if you're in a hurry and very particular about your color and a quick way to cool your wax can be extremely helpful.

CHAPTER 13
Adding Dye

The natural coloring of beeswax is amazing all on its own, but there are some instances where you may want to dye your wax for specific effects.

White Beeswax vs Yellow Beeswax

When using dye, the base color of the wax is extremely important. I always start with a white beeswax base as I find the color is more consistent between batches and also more stable over time.

Since yellow wax is already, well, yellow, it will cause changes in the final color of your wax. I won't get too crazy with color theory here. Yellow is one of the primary colors, so it can be leveraged to create other hues. For example, adding a bit of red will make your final result kind of orangey. This won't always be apparent right away either. When I started dyeing wax, I had a beautiful green that turned muddy and gross after a few weeks. Also, since beeswax color can change from batch to batch, your dye recipes won't be as reliable if you are planning to go this route.

Creating a New Color

I have a lot of fun mixing new colors. A brand-new recipe can be a bit of a pain if you're in a hurry and very particular about your color, and a quick way to cool your wax can be extremely helpful.

MATERIALS:
- 1 – Double boiler setup (see Chapter 6 for instructions)
- Beeswax (white or yellow—I always use white)
- Dye (see Chapter 7 for more information)
- Scale
- Stir stick (popsicle sticks, chopsticks, and skewers work very well)
- Pen and paper to document your recipe (optional)
- Shallow mold (optional)
- Aluminum foil (optional)
- Cool place such as a refrigerator or freezer to quickly cool your test wax (optional)

INSTRUCTIONS:

1. Carefully weigh out some beeswax and place it in your double boiler (I like to work with 50–100 g (1.5–3.5 oz) at a time when testing a new recipe).
2. Record the amount if you're planning to save the recipe (when testing a new recipe, I like to document the wax weight and the dye weight on two separate lines in case I need to add more of either to get the right color).
3. Set up your double boiler with the beeswax on the stove on low-medium heat.
4. Weigh your dye (I like to add very little to start—usually less than 1 g (0.05 oz)—as it's very easy to go overboard!).
5. Record the dye amount.
6. When the wax is completely melted, add the dye and mix thoroughly.
7. Pour a small quantity of wax into a shallow mold or onto a piece of aluminum foil. Alternatively, remove the wax from heat and allow to cool.
8. If using a refrigerator or freezer, place the sample of wax (or the entire container of hot wax) in until completely cooled. The wax will look very dark in liquid form and very light when it has solidified but still warm, so it's important to completely cool the wax to ensure you get a good indicator of the final color.
9. If you're color isn't quite right, remelt the wax, adding small quantities of wax (to lighten the color) or dye (to darken the color). Record the additional weights of wax and dye as you go.
10. Repeat steps 4–9 until you achieve the desired color.

I like to keep a test notebook with all of my color experiments. Sometimes, I write the recipes I want to keep separately in a clean notebook so I don't have to add up the numbers or wonder which numbers are correct each time I make the recipe. It may also be helpful to include color swatches in your notebook to remind yourself of the color (small dots of wax cooled on aluminum foil work well) or keep a note with leftover wax (I organize mine in bags).

Wick and Dye

It's sometimes necessary to change the wick size for dyed candles. For example, I've gone up a wick size for dark dyed tealight candles to get them to burn properly. When you come up with a new color, make sure you test the wicks you are using!

Layering Colors

A fun project idea is to layer colors. If you are using undyed wax with dyed wax or darkly dyed wax with light dyed wax, you may run into some color bleed. To minimize this, I like to work with wax at the coolest temperature possible while still getting a good pour. A lower pour temperature results in less immediate mixing of layers; however, it will not prevent bleeding over time.

Things to Watch For

Overdoing the color—remember your melting vat is only so large, so I like to start with very small quantities of wax and dye. That way, if I go overboard on the dye, I have plenty of room to dilute the color.

Color change—sometimes the color of the wax will change over the course of a few weeks. For new dye combinations, I like to let them sit for at least a few weeks before confirming the final recipe. Some colors will change months after creation!

TIPS AND TRICKS

Once you've perfected your recipe, it's always a good idea to check back on the color when you use the recipe again in the future. I like to keep a small dyed piece of wax handy as a reference and spot check future batches of colored wax against it.

I like to keep a notebook for when I'm creating new recipes.

Adding Scent

To keep the scent at its most potent, I always add my oil right before pouring. At this point, it's very important to stir the mixture very well. Otherwise, the oil will be unevenly distributed.

CHAPTER 14
Adding Scent

Personally, I think beeswax is amazing on its own; however, sometimes it's nice to add a different scent for a different experience. I have used both essential and fragrance oils successfully and unsuccessfully. I've found the most important thing to pay attention to in choosing your scents is to select scents that will work with the natural scent of beeswax. I remember trying out a scent called 'Sexy Cherry' once – I was looking for a cherry scent and this was the best I could find. Sexy Cherry really didn't smell like cherry to me. It was very musky and I was not a fan from the time I opened the bottle. Mixing the heavy musk scent with the natural slightly sweet beeswax smell made it even worse in my opinion. Needless to say, after the test batch was done, I never used that scent again.

Essential Oils

Essential oils can be a bit more finicky to work with as I've found the scent will dissipate much quicker than with a fragrance oil. That said, I tend to use the same ratio of scent to wax in both cases.

I test my candles in a fairly small room with a low ceiling. I also prefer a more subtle scent in the room. This is directly related to how I create my recipe. I normally use approximately 5% essential oil in my candles. Now, each essential oil behaves differently, and the potency will vary based on the oils used and ratios. For example, I find the Chai blend I created to have a more significant scent throw and a stronger scent overall than the London Fog blend.

Fragrance Oils

Again, potency varies from oil to oil in the fragrance world. For example, I've used a few different floral scents and found some have a great scent throw, and others are hardly noticeable despite all of them smelling wonderful when they are freshly made.

Creating a New Oil Blend

I started my scent journey using pre-made or single scents (for example, lavender essential oil or mulled wine fragrance oil). Once you're comfortable with that, though, it's always fun to start creating your own. Perhaps you have a favorite blend that would be even better with just a bit of cinnamon added to it. Or you can get even more adventurous and create your own blend from scratch. When I'm creating a new oil blend, I carefully document the quantities of each component I'm using by weight. I'm always aware of how the resulting blend will work with the scent of beeswax. I like to keep a notebook in the workshop for when I'm creating new recipes. Each new color, scent, and product gets a new page where I document changes and make notes on what works and what doesn't.

So, let's get down to creating a scented candle.

> To keep the scent at its most potent, I always add my oil right before pouring. At this point, it's very important to stir the mixture very well. Otherwise, the oil will be unevenly distributed.

MATERIALS:
- 1 – Double boiler setup (see Chapter 6 for instructions)
- Beeswax
- Wick
- Container (optional—I like to make a small batch of tealights when I'm testing a new recipe)
- Scent (fragrance or essential oil; see Chapter 8 for more information)
- Small container to hold measured scent (I like to use old glass yogurt containers or small sauce bowls. Some plastics react to certain scents or pick up the scent leading to possible cross-contamination)
- Scale
- Stir stick (popsicle sticks, chopsticks, and skewers work very well)
- Pen and paper to document your recipe (optional)
- Aluminum foil (optional)

INSTRUCTIONS:
1. Carefully weigh out 5 g (0.2 oz) of scent into the small container.
2. Record the amount if you're planning to save the recipe (I like to document wax weight and scent weight on two separate lines in case I need to add more of either one).
3. Weigh out 100 g (3.5 oz) of beeswax and place it in your double boiler. (To determine how much beeswax you'll be using, the math is easy—
(2 x amount of scent) x 10 = amount of beeswax needed. If you have 5 g of scent,
(2 x 5 g) x 10 = (10 g) x 10 = 100 g beeswax).
4. Record the amount if you're planning to save the recipe (I do this every time just in case!).
5. When wax is completely melted, add the scent and stir VERY well.
6. Pour a couple of test candles.
7. Allow candles to cool.
8. Test your candles.

Things to Watch For

Too much oil—oils may change the composition of the mixture enough that you may need a different wick. In my experience, I haven't had to adjust wick sizes at 5% oil, but it may be worth experimenting if you run into issues.

Unmixed oil—it's crucial to ensure the oil is very well blended with the beeswax. If it is not blended well enough, multiple candles from the same batch will have inconsistent scent (specifically in the case of tealights because they are so small!).

TIPS AND TRICKS

For my most popular scents, I make extra wax beyond what I need for the day's project. The extra is poured into silicone ice cube molds and stored in labeled Ziploc bags once cooled. That way, if a small project comes up or I need a few extra candles, I have pre-mixed wax ready to go at a moment's notice (this is especially helpful if I forget to re-order a scent, or an order is delayed!). It's important to minimize the number of times you reheat scented wax, however, as the scent will degrade with repeated heating.

It may also be helpful to include recipes in your notebook.

Troubleshooting

To fix a candle that has already cracked, use a heat gun to melt the wax and fill in the cracks or melt the candle down and try again.

CHAPTER 15
Troubleshooting

Now that you have some experience under your belt, you may be wondering what to do if things go wrong! In this section, we'll look at some common issues you may run into, why they happen, and what you can do to fix it.

Section 3: Troubleshooting & Testing

Cracking

WHAT IS IT?
Cracks appear on your candle commonly near the wick.

WHY DOES IT HAPPEN?
The wax cooled too quickly, or the container was not filled completely.

HOW DO I FIX IT?
To prevent this from happening, make sure the ambient temperature and pouring temperature are appropriate (a warmer room prevents the candle from cooling too quickly, and the melted wax temperature should be optimal for beeswax).

Make sure your container is filled completely. I most commonly run into this issue with tealights when there is not enough wax in the cup—make sure you can see the meniscus above the top of the container.

To fix a candle that has already cracked, use a heat gun to melt the wax and fill in the cracks (you may need to add more liquid wax) or melt the candle down and try again.

Shrinkage

WHAT IS IT?
The candle pulls away from the container you've poured it into.

WHY DOES IT HAPPEN?
It's natural! Beeswax shrinks as it cools, pulling it away from the edges of the container.

HOW DO I FIX IT?
Beeswax will shrink as it cools, so pouring at a cooler temperature can somewhat help, although you likely won't be able to completely eradicate it.

To fix the issue on a candle you've just made, you can try heating up the vessel until the wax fills in the gaps. Sometimes this works for me, and sometimes it doesn't.

Leave it.

Visible Rings

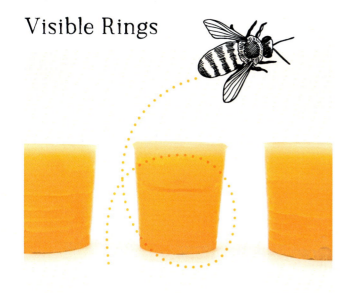

Increase the temperature of the wax before pouring.

WHAT IS IT?
The candle has ridges on it when it comes out of a mold or visible through the clear sides of a container.

WHY DOES IT HAPPEN?
The wax was poured at too cool of a temperature. The wax started cooling as it was poured, which allowed formation of the rings.

HOW DO I FIX IT?
Increase the temperature of the wax before pouring.

Testing

Once your candles are finished, it's time to test!

CHAPTER 16
Testing

It's important to test your candles to make sure they burn as expected. In creating my candles, I like to maximize the amount of wax used up (minimize wax waste), ensure the candle burns beautifully (with an appropriate flame size and burn rate), and prevent dripping as much as possible.

PREPARING FOR A TEST

When I first started testing candles, I tested a variety of wicks for the same candle at the same time. Once I figured out which wicks worked well for different-sized candles, I used the knowledge to make a better estimation of wicks that would work well for similarly sized candles. This has worked out well for me so far! The method I share below is taken from how I burn tested when I first started making candles.

For an accurate test, here are some tips on preparing your candles:

- Create 3–5 of the same candles with your best estimate of which wicks may work well. I like to use a recommended size and then choose 1–2 sizes below as well as 1–2 sizes above.
- Keep as many variables the same as possible (type of container if applicable, make the candles at the same time).
- If possible, use beeswax from the same batch (burn behavior can vary between batches!).
- If possible, make the candles at the same time using wax that has been heated to the same temperature. For example, I will prepare the different wicks for tealights and pour them all at once.
- Label the candles with wick sizes. For candles with longer wicks, I like to put tape around the wick and write the size on the tape with a pen or marker. For tealights, I write the wick size on the bottom or side of the tealight cup.

Conducting a Test

Once your candles are finished, it's time to test! Make sure you have sufficient time to complete your test in one block of time (up to four hours or so at a time).

1. Set up the test environment.
    - Put test candles on a heat-resistant surface leaving room in between candles to breathe—a few inches between each candle is great.
    - Ensure all candles are clearly labeled. If you have written the wick size on the bottom of a tealight cup, create a second label so you can easily see it as you proceed with the test burn.
    - Trim wicks if necessary.
    - Keep candles in a suitable area for your test. If I'm testing wicks, I like to keep them in an area with little air disturbance. If I'm testing for scent throw, I'll test them in the environment they are being tested for and where they will most likely be used (small or large room, on a shelf or table, etc.).

2. Prepare to record your results.
    - Have a timer or alarm ready to set (such as on your phone) so you can check your candles at regular time intervals (I like to check at half hour or hour intervals depending on the candle and what I'm testing for).

- Have a pen and paper or electronic device handy to record your observations. The sample testing table on page 124 is one example of how you can set up your test data.
- Set the timer for your next check-in.
- At the allocated time, record your observations for each candle.

3. Set the timer for your next check-in.
4. At each check-in, record:
   - Melt pool width.
   - Melt pool depth.
   - Whether there is soot on the container edge and how much.
   - Flame height—approximately how high is the flame? If you want to be more precise, feel free to use a ruler to measure it more closely.
   - Flame movement—is the flame steady or flickering? Note if there is an air disturbance in the area as well.
   - Mushrooming behavior—does the wick have what looks like the top of a mushroom? Is it causing the wick to tip over or dropping carbon deposits in the wax pool?
   - Any other observations.

5. Repeat steps 1–3 until the candle has been burning for the length of time of your choosing.
   - It's best to limit candles to burning for no more than four hours at a time.

6. If needed, conduct additional burn tests until the candle is finished.
   - Let the candle cool for at least five hours before running your next test cycle.[xxvi]

In testing my candles, I like to maximize the amount of wax used up.

Table 2: Sample Testing Table for Wicks

BURN TEST 1 FOR 3X3" YELLOW BEESWAX PILLAR

DATE: OCTOBER 1, 2023

Wick Size	Time Elapsed	Melt Pool Width	Melt Pool Depth	Soot on Container Edge? How much?	Flame Height	Flame Movement	Mushrooming?	Other Comments
#1	30 min							
	60 min							
	90 min							
	120 min							
#2	30 min							
	60 min							
	90 min							
	120 min							
#3	30 min							
	60 min							
	90 min							
	120 min							

Interpreting the Test Results

Here's what I like to look for when I'm testing candles:

- Tunneling
  - The first burn of a candle is called the memory burn. If the wax pool has not reached the ideal width before being extinguished, future wax pools may be too small wasting the wax at the edges.
- Mushrooming behavior
  - Mushrooming occurs when the wax is unable to burn quickly enough to keep up with the burn rate of the wick. The top of the wick will look similar to a mushroom.
  - If the wick has mushroomed and is tipping over or dropping carbon deposits in the wax pool, the wick size may need to be reduced.
  - Mushrooming can also occur if the wick has not been trimmed before lighting. I always trim wicks before I light candles.

Example of wick mushrooming.

Example of what a good burn should look like.

- Moderate burn rate: melt pool should be 6–13 mm (¼–½") deep and to the edges of the candle within 1 hour multiplied by the width of the candle (a 3" candle should have a full melt pool within three hours)
    - Melt pool depth will vary throughout the life of the candle.
    - Melt pool width will also depend on the type of behavior you are looking for and the type of candle.
    - Melt pool width behavior will change with each burn cycle on longer burning candles, so it's important to observe throughout the life of the candle.
- Moderate flame size: 13–50 mm (½–2") tall depending on the candle
- Minimize dripping over the edges

Verifying the Test

Once you've decided on a wick, it can be helpful to test a few more candles (three or so) to make sure the burn behavior is consistent. I also like to spot test my candles once in a while to make sure the wick is still working, especially as I work with beeswax from different batches.

Calculating Burn Time

To calculate the estimated burn time of your candle, you can time the burn of your candle for its entire burn life or calculate it based on a series of test burns.

Full Burn Calculation

In this calculation, you will completely burn the candle you are testing. Here are the steps:

1. Trim the wick if needed.
2. Light the candle. Record the start time.
3. When you extinguish the candle, record the end time. Remember to extinguish your candle at least every four hours and allow it to cool completely.
4. Continue steps 1 to 3 until the candle is finished.
5. Add up the total number of hours the candle burned.

I like to conduct a few full burn tests and average the results. The final burn time I assign is always slightly less than my test results to account for variations in the burning environment. It may be helpful to burn your candle in different situations that reflect how it will be burned in real life as part of your testing process.

Partial Burn Calculation

In this calculation, you will use the weight of the candle to calculate how long the candle is estimated to last. Here are the steps:

1. Record the weight of the wax used in the candle. If you are using a container, be sure to measure

the weight of the empty container before making your candle—we are only interested in wax weight here!
(total weight − container weight = wax weight)

2. Trim the wick if needed.
3. Light the candle. Record the start time.
4. When you extinguish the candle, record the end time. Remember to extinguish your candle at most every four hours.
5. When the candle has cooled completely, re-weigh the candle. Record the new wax weight (remember total weight − container weight = new wax weight for container candles).
6. Calculate the total amount of wax used.
(wax weight − new wax weight = wax used)
7. Calculate how much burns are expected.
(wax weight / wax used = expected burns)
8. Calculate burn time [expected burns * (burn end time − burn start time) = burn time]

There are many factors that can affect the accuracy of this number, so I like to err on the side of caution and assume a lower burn time than the calculation result.

It may be helpful to burn your candle in different situations that reflect how it will be burned in real life as part of your testing process.

Creative Candles

I suggest being very careful when adding flammable organic material to your candles.

128

CHAPTER 17
Creative Candles

Now that you know the basics of candle making, let your creativity flow as you take your candles to the next level! There are limitless ways to add your own unique touch.

Section 4: The Finishing Touch

Add More Wax

Beeswax sheets are a quick and easy way to add wax decorations to your candles. Whether you create a work of art on the side of a pillar candle or create a surprise on the top of a container candle, sheets are easy to work with.

If you don't have sheets or want to create a different type of art, fondant molds (used for fondant and cake decorating) can be used with melted beeswax to create add-ons for your candle. You can also drip small beads of wax onto a piece of aluminum foil and form them into shapes by hand.

Transfer Candles

Adding pictures to candles is simple and only requires a few extra supplies: tissue paper, a printer, and wax paper.

1. Print your image on tissue paper. I like to tape a piece of tissue to a regular piece of paper to give the printer a more structured piece of material to print on.
2. Cut around the image as close to the picture as possible.
3. Place the picture where you'd like it on the outside of the candle, smoothing the tissue as much as possible.
4. Place a piece of wax paper (if it is only waxed on one side, face waxed side toward the candle) over the tissue. I like to make sure the wax paper is big enough to wrap around the entire candle with room to hold it closed with my hand (you can also use binder clips to keep both hands free!).
5. Using a hair dryer or heat gun, heat the wax paper using a back and forth motion until the image shows through the wax paper. Be careful not to melt the candle or burn your fingers!
6. Carefully peel off the wax paper.
7. If any spots of tissue haven't adhered to the candle, replace the wax paper and melt again.

Pressed Flowers or Other Add Ons

I suggest being very careful when adding flammable organic material to your candles. I do not recommend decorating the top of your candle to reduce fire risk. When I use organic material on my candles, I tend to use them on candles designed not to burn completely through such as pillars. That way, the shell of the candle can be saved for future use (such as burning a tealight inside as a luminary while preserving the outer decoration of the candle). Pressed leaves and flowers can add more natural beauty to your candles.

I've also used cinnamon sticks to create a reusable seasonal candle cover for the holidays. Using a 3" candle as a template, I hot glue cinnamon sticks together and wrap them in decorative jute or hemp twine. Once the candle is burned, it can be replaced and used again and again. The cinnamon sticks give off a gentle cinnamon scent as they warm when the candle burns.

Carved Candles

Another way to add interest to your candle is to carve a design into the wax. This works particularly well with pillar candles designed to leave a bit of wax on the outside so the design can be enjoyed again and again. It takes a bit of practice to make sure you don't carve too deep (and of course to make sure the wicking is correct to give you the effect you're looking for!).

Painted Candles

Adding paint can take a candle from ordinary to extraordinary with a few brush strokes. Whether you're into painting simple patterns, elaborate scenes, or letting kids go crazy, painting the outside of your candle can add a very personal artistic touch. As with the pressed flowers, I don't recommend decorating the top of your candle as it can pose a fire hazard.

I don't recommend decorating the top of your candle as it can pose a fire hazard.

Gift & Packaging Ideas

Add some ribbon, twine, string, or cord on its own or over a piece of scrapbooking paper or fabric.

CHAPTER 19
Gift & Packaging Ideas

You've made some gorgeous candles and you're now ready to share them with the world! Whether you've decided to share your new skill with friends and family or start a new business, the next step is packaging! In this section, I'll share some ideas on how you can package your candles on their own or in gift sets. Let's get started!

Single Candles

For rolled candles, I sometimes like to loop the wick to make it look a bit fancier. You can even go one step further and thread a tag on the wick before you start rolling. Another option is to leave extra wick at the top to tie on a tag later.

With container candles, tie a paper tag around the container with ribbon, twine, string, or cord. Sticker labels also work well. You can get stickers custom made, use existing stickers you love (large 3D stickers on top of a mason jar can work well), or print your own labels at home.

Creating wraps for your candles can also add a finishing touch to your candle. Add some ribbon, twine, string, or cord on its own or over a piece of scrapbooking paper or fabric.

Gift Sets

Individual candles make fantastic gifts, but sometimes you may need a larger gift. Putting together a selection of candles can cover a variety of candle needs for the recipient and look impressive at the same time!

For taper candles, tie them together with ribbon, twine, string, or cord to keep them together. Adding a fabric or paper wrap to these can work really well too.

For fancier gift giving, a large woven basket can look great filled with basket filler, a selection of candles, and wrapped up in cellophane with curling ribbon.

Another option for gift giving is to use a box with tissue or filler either wrapped in cellophane or tied up with a nice ribbon, twine, or string.

For the eco-conscious, wrapping using a furoshiki cloth is a unique way to give a gift while reducing waste. There are so many amazing ways to fold furoshiki cloth. It's easy to make your own custom size in the fabric of your choice whether you have a sewing machine or choose to use pinking shears.

HOW TO MAKE FUROSHIKI CLOTH WITHOUT A SEWING MACHINE:

1. Choose your fabric.
2. Measure a square in the size of your choice.
3. Cut the square using pinking shears.

HOW TO MAKE A FUROSHIKI CLOTH WITH A SERGER:

1. Choose your fabric.
2. Measure a square in the size of your choice.
3. Cut the square with fabric scissors.
4. Set the machine to do a rolled hem.
5. Stitch the edges of the fabric.

Wrapping with traditional wrapping paper is also an option. Many of the candles I make have odd shapes and sizes, so I like to find a box and carefully wrap the candles inside the box (this is a fantastic method for shipping gifts as well!). From there, you just have to wrap the entire box!

Complementary Gift Sets

Your gift sets don't only need to include candles! Think of a theme for your gift and create a gift set accordingly. Here are some ideas to get you started:

- A tea or coffee themed gift basket including a new mug, their favourite tea or coffee, a candle, and some honey
- A birthday set including birthday candles and sweet treats
- At home spa sets including candles, bath goodies, and lotion
- Meditation sets including candles and a stone, singing bowl, cushion, or music
- Housewarming set including candles and candle holders, kitchen towels, and a freshly baked dish of food

- Dorm set including candles and candle holders and a plant
- Gift set around the theme of a party

Gift Extras

Giving a handmade gift is appreciated, but sometimes it's not quite enough. If the person you're gifting already has a lot of candles or you notice something they don't have that would make their life easier, candle accessories can be added to your gift as well. Here are some ideas for candle paraphernalia that can be added to your gift:

- Snuffer
- Wick scissors
- Candle plate (for pillars)
- Beautiful candle holder (for tapers, tealights, or votives)
- A lighter or set of matches

Final Thoughts

The world of beeswax candle making is like Pandora's box—once you've opened it, there is a never-ending world of learning open to you. I hope this book has provided an excellent starting point on your journey into the world of beeswax candles. Best wishes as you continue on your candle-making adventures!

> The world of beeswax candle making is like Pandora's box—once you've opened it, there is a never-ending world of learning open to you.

Appendix A: Does the direction of the V in square braid wick affect burn behavior in dipped taper candles?

Hypothesis

The direction of the V in square braid wick will change the burn behavior in beeswax dipped taper candles.

Procedure

1. Make 5 pairs of dipped tapers. One candle in each pair will have the V open to the top while the other has the V open to the bottom.
2. Measure (height, base circumference, and base diameter) and weigh (grams) each candle.
3. Set up candles in holders. Trim wicks to approximately 0.5 cm (¼").
4. Burn candles for two hours. At each 30 minute interval:
   1. Take one picture of the entire experiment including all candles.
   2. Take a picture of the flame of each candle. Ensure they are clearly identified.
   3. Record burn characteristics (see charts below).
5. Extinguish the candles at the end of the two hour burn period.
6. Cool for at least two hours.
7. Record new height and weight for each candle.
8. Repeat steps 3-7 twice more (total of three sets of data documenting burn time 0-2 hours, 2-4 hours, and 4-6 hours).

Data

A candles have the V open to the bottom

B candles have the V open to the top

The number denotes the pairs that were dipped together.

Table 3: Candle Specifications Before Starting Tests

Candle Code	Weight (g)	Height (cm)	Circumference (cm)*	Diameter (cm)*
1A	45.42	18.8	6.6	1.8
1B	47.18	18.6	6.7	1.8
2A	49.27	19.8	6.5	1.7
2B	48.83	19.7	6.4	1.6
3A	45.53	19.0	6.4	1.7
3B	46.06	19.5	6.5	1.6
4A	46.06	19.2	6.4	1.6
4B	45.70	19.6	6.4	1.6
5A	44.88	18.5	6.5	1.6
5B	44.88	18.5	6.5	1.6

* Measurements were taken at the base of the candle

Burn Test 1 (0-2 Hours Total Burn Time)

Test Date: October 30, 2023

Table 4: Burn Behavior for Burn Test 1

Candle	Time	Flame Height	Flame Movement	Mushrooming?	Other notes
1A	30 min	~3 cm	Good	Small mushroom	Long length of wick exposed within flame (~1.5 cm)
	60 min	~3 cm	Good	Mushroom progressed	Long length of wick exposed within flame (~1.5 cm)
	90 min	~3 cm	Good	No	Long length of wick exposed within flame (~1.5 cm)
	120 min	~3 cm	Good	No	Long length of wick exposed within flame (~2 cm)
1B	30 min	~3 cm	Good	No	Wick exposed ~1 cm
	60 min	~3 cm	Good	No	Wick exposed ~1 cm
	90 min	~3 cm	Good	No	Wick exposed ~1 cm
	120 min	~3 cm	Good	No	Wick exposed ~1 cm
2A	30 min	~3 cm	Good	No	Long length of wick exposed within flame (~1.5 cm)
	60 min	~3 cm	Good	Quite significant mushroom	Long length of wick exposed within flame (~1.5 cm)
	90 min	~3 cm	Good	No	Long length of wick exposed within flame (~1.5 cm)
	120 min	~3 cm	Good	Some mushrooming	Long length of wick exposed within flame (~1.5 cm)
2B	30 min	~3 cm	Good	No	Wick exposed ~1 cm
	60 min	~3 cm	Good	No	Wick exposed ~1 cm
	90 min	~3 cm	Good	No	Wick exposed ~1 cm
	120 min	~3 cm	Good	No	Wick exposed ~1 cm
3A	30 min	~3 cm	Good	No	Long length of wick exposed within flame (~1.5 cm); small amount of carbon (?) in wax pool
	60 min	~3 cm	Good	No	Long length of wick exposed within flame (~1.5 cm); small amount of carbon (?) in wax pool
	90 min	~3 cm	Good	Small mushroom	Long length of wick exposed within flame (~1.5 cm); small amount of carbon (?) in wax pool

	120 min	~3 cm	Good	Small mushroom	Long length of wick exposed within flame (~1.5 cm); small amount of carbon (?) in wax pool
3B	30 min	~3 cm	Good	No	Wick exposed ~1 cm
	60 min	~3 cm	Good	No	Wick exposed ~1 cm
	90 min	~3 cm	Good	No	Wick exposed ~1 cm
	120 min	~3 cm	Good	No	Wick exposed ~1 cm
4A	30 min	~3 cm	Good	No	Long length of wick exposed within flame (~1.5 cm)
	60 min	~3 cm	Good	Small mushroom	Long length of wick exposed within flame (~1.5 cm)
	90 min	~3 cm	Good	Small mushroom	Long length of wick exposed within flame (~1.5 cm)
	120 min	~3 cm	Good	Small mushroom	Long length of wick exposed within flame (~1.5 cm)
4B	30 min	~3 cm	Good	No	Wick exposed ~1 cm
	60 min	~3 cm	Good	No	Wick exposed ~1 cm
	90 min	~3 cm	Good	No	Wick exposed ~1 cm
	120 min	~3 cm	Good	No	Wick exposed ~1 cm
5A	30 min	~3 cm	Good	No	Long length of wick exposed within flame (~1.5 cm)
	60 min	~3 cm	Good	Significant mushroom	Long length of wick exposed within flame (~2 cm)
	90 min	~3 cm	Good	Significant mushroom	Long length of wick exposed within flame (~1.5 cm)
	120 min	~3 cm	Good	Small mushroom	Long length of wick exposed within flame (~1.5 cm)
5B	30 min	~3 cm	Good	No	Wick exposed ~1 cm
	60 min	~3 cm	Good	No	Wick exposed ~1 cm
	90 min	~3 cm	Good	No	Wick exposed ~1 cm
	120 min	~3 cm	Good	No	Wick exposed ~1 cm

Burn Test 2 (2-4 Hours Total Burn Time)

Test Date: October 31, 2023

Table 5: Candle Height and Weight Prior to Burn Test 2

Candle Code	Weight (g)	Height (cm)
1A	34.59	12.4
1B	36.04	12.4
2A	38.42	13.5
2B	37.67	13.7
3A	34.78	12.6
3B	34.82	12.5
4A	35.59	12.9
4B	34.66	12.9
5A	33.86	12.1
5B	34.31	12.3

Table 6: Burn Behavior for Burn Test 2

Candle	Time	Flame Height	Flame Movement	Mushrooming?	Other notes
1A	30 min	~3 cm	Good	No	Wick exposed ~1 cm
	60 min	~3 cm	Good	Small	Wick exposed ~1.5 cm
	90 min	~3 cm	Good	Small	Wick exposed ~1.5 cm
	120 min	~3 cm	Good	No	Wick exposed ~1.5 cm
1B	30 min	~3 cm	Good	No	Wick exposed ~1 cm; dripped a bit
	60 min	~3 cm	Good	No	Wick exposed ~1 cm; no new dripping
	90 min	~3 cm	Good	No	Wick exposed ~1 cm; no new dripping
	120 min	~3 cm	Good	No	Wick exposed ~1 cm; no new dripping
2A	30 min	~3 cm	Good	No	Wick exposed ~1 cm
	60 min	~3 cm	Good	Moderate	Wick exposed ~1.5 cm
	90 min	~3 cm	Good	Moderate	Wick exposed ~1.5 cm
	120 min	~3 cm	Good	Small	Wick exposed ~1.5 cm
2B	30 min	~3 cm	Good	No	Wick exposed ~1 cm; dripped a bit
	60 min	~3 cm	Good	No	Wick exposed ~1 cm; no new dripping

	90 min	~3 cm	Good	No	Wick exposed ~1 cm; no new dripping
	120 min	~3 cm	Good	No	Wick exposed ~1 cm; no new dripping
3A	30 min	~3 cm	Good	No	Wick exposed ~1 cm
	60 min	~3 cm	Good	No	Wick exposed ~1.5 cm
	90 min	~3 cm	Good	No	Wick exposed ~1.5 cm
	120 min	~3 cm	Good	Moderate	Wick exposed ~1.5 cm
3B	30 min	~3 cm	Good	No	Wick exposed ~1 cm; dripped quite a bit
	60 min	~3 cm	Good	No	Wick exposed ~1 cm; dripped a bit; tilted
	90 min	~3 cm	Good	No	Wick exposed ~1 cm; no new drips; tilted
	120 min	~3 cm	Good	No	Wick exposed ~1 cm; significant new drips; tilted
4A	30 min	~3 cm	Good	No	Wick exposed ~1 cm
	60 min	~3 cm	Good	No	Wick exposed ~1.5 cm
	90 min	~3 cm	Good	Small	Wick exposed ~1.5 cm
	120 min	~3 cm	Good	No	Wick exposed ~1.5 cm
4B	30 min	~3 cm	Good	No	Wick exposed ~1 cm
	60 min	~3 cm	Good	No	Wick exposed ~1 cm
	90 min	~3 cm	Good	No	Wick exposed ~1 cm
	120 min	~3 cm	Good	No	Wick exposed ~1 cm
5A	30 min	~3 cm	Good	Moderate	Wick exposed ~1 cm; dripped a bit
	60 min	~3 cm	Good	No	Wick exposed ~1 cm; no new dripping
	90 min	~3 cm	Good	No	Wick exposed ~1 cm; no new dripping
	120 min	~3 cm	Good	Moderate	Wick exposed ~1 cm; no new dripping
5B	30 min	~3 cm	Good	No	Wick exposed ~1 cm; dripped a lot; quite tipped over
	60 min	~3 cm	Good	No	Wick exposed ~1 cm; lots more dripping; quite tipped over. Extinguished
	90 min				N/A extinguished
	120 min				N/A extinguished

NOTE: Dripping candles don't appear to be fully upright.

Burn Test 3 (4-6 Hours Total Burn Time)

Test Date: November 1, 2023

Table 7: Candle Height and Weight Prior to Burn Test 3

Candle Code	Weight (g)	Height (cm)
1A	24.02	8.5
1B	25.32	8.3
2A	27.64	9.6
2B	26.14	9.1
3A	24.31	8.6
3B	14.15	5.0
4A	24.60	8.6
4B	23.93	8.6
5A	22.78	7.9
5B	9.73	3.2

Table 8: Burn Behavior for Burn Test 3

Candle	Time	Flame Height	Flame Movement	Mushrooming?	Other notes
1A	30 min	~3 cm	Good	No	Wick exposed ~1 cm
	60 min	~3 cm	Good	No	Wick exposed ~2 cm
	90 min	~3 cm	Good	Small	Wick exposed ~2 cm
	120 min	~3 cm	Good	No	Wick exposed ~2 cm
1B	30 min	~3 cm	Good	No	Wick exposed ~1 cm
	60 min	~3 cm	Good	No	Wick exposed ~1 cm
	90 min	~3 cm	Good	No	Wick exposed ~1 cm
	120 min	~3 cm	Good	No	Wick exposed ~1 cm
2A	30 min	~3 cm	Good	No	Wick exposed ~1 cm
	60 min	~3 cm	Good	No	Wick exposed ~1.5 cm
	90 min	~3 cm	Good	No	Wick exposed ~1.5 cm
	120 min	~3 cm	Good	Large	Wick exposed ~1.5 cm
2B	30 min	~3 cm	Good	No	Wick exposed ~1 cm
	60 min	~3 cm	Good	No	Wick exposed ~1 cm

	90 min	~3 cm	Good	No	Wick exposed ~1 cm
	120 min	~3 cm	Good	No	Wick exposed ~1 cm
3A	30 min	~3 cm	Good	No	Wick exposed ~1 cm; seems to be a fault on the wick – small protrusion
	60 min	~3 cm	Good	No	Wick exposed ~1.5 cm; wax dripping significantly
	90 min	~3 cm	Good	No	Wick exposed ~2 cm; wax drip stopped
	120 min	~3 cm	Good	Moderate	Wick exposed ~2 cm; wax drip stopped
3B	30 min	~3 cm	Good	No	Wick exposed ~1 cm
	60 min	~3 cm	Good	No	Wick exposed ~1 cm; extinguished due to size
	90 min	N/A extinguished			
	120 min				
4A	30 min	~3 cm	Good	No	Wick exposed ~1 cm
	60 min	~3 cm	Good	No	Wick exposed ~1.5 cm
	90 min	~3 cm	Good	No	Wick exposed ~2 cm
	120 min	~3 cm	Good	No	Wick exposed ~2 cm
4B	30 min	~3 cm	Good	No	Wick exposed ~1 cm
	60 min	~3 cm	Good	No	Wick exposed ~1 cm
	90 min	~3 cm	Good	No	Wick exposed ~1 cm
	120 min	~3 cm	Good	No	Wick exposed ~1 cm
5A	30 min	~3 cm	Good	No	Wick exposed ~1 cm
	60 min	~3 cm	Good	Moderate	Wick exposed ~2 cm
	90 min	~3 cm	Good	Small	Wick exposed ~2 cm
	120 min	~3 cm	Good	No	Wick exposed ~2 cm
5B	30 min	N/A too small			
	60 min				
	90 min				
	120 min				

NOTE: Dripping candles don't appear to be fully upright.

Table 9: Final Candle Height and Weight

Candle Code	Weight (g)	Height (cm)
1A	13.08	4.5
1B	14.28	4.7
2A	16.77	5.7
2B	14.49	5.0
3A	10.50	3.8
3B	8.07	2.8
4A	13.91	4.8
4B	13.23	4.7
5A	11.82	3.9
5B	9.73	3.2

Results

To determine whether the candles were consistent in behavior, the differences in height and weight of candles in the same condition – V open to bottom or V open to top – were graphed (Figures 1-4).

Figure 1: Height Changes Over Time for V Open to Bottom

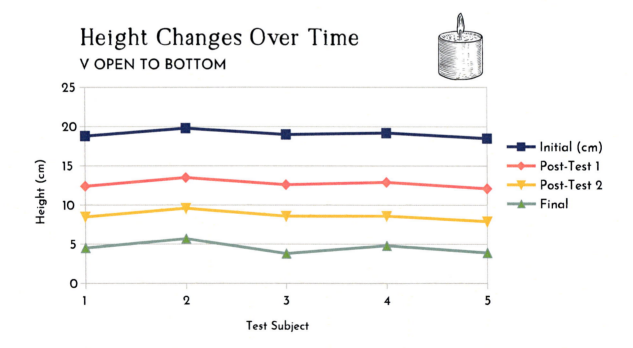

Figure 2: Height Changes Over Time for V Open to Top

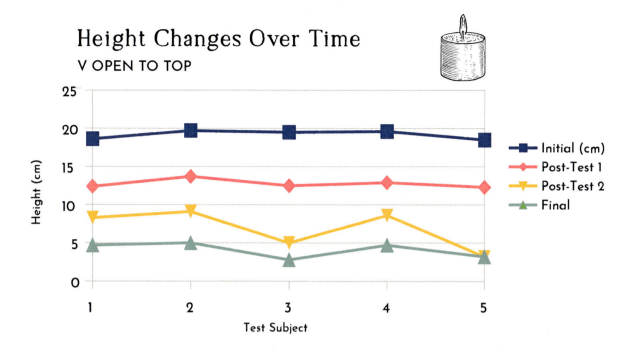

Figure 3: Weight Changes Over Time for V Open to Bottom

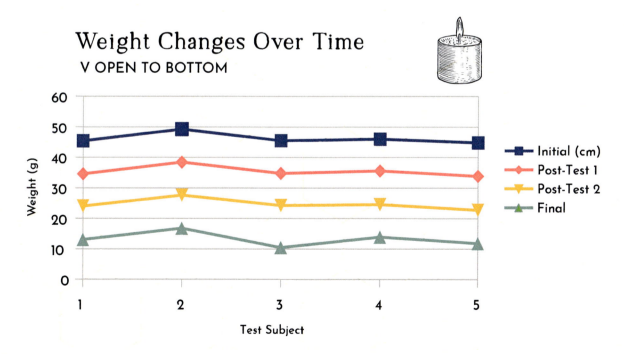

Figure 4: Weight Changes Over Time for V Open to Top

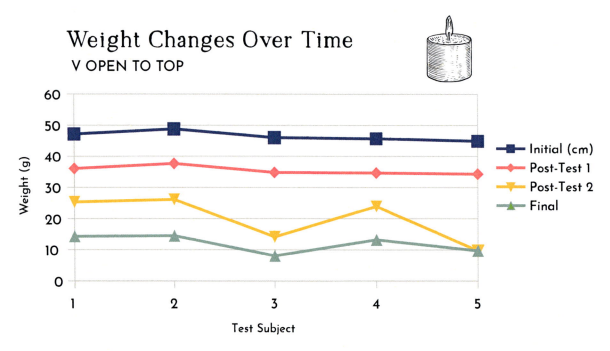

Based on these graphs, it appears the burn behavior is consistent across both conditions. Candles 3 and 5 in the V open to top condition dripped significantly, which accounts for the drastic changes in height and weight in the Post Test 2 data (Figures 2 and 4). Candle 5 was too short to continue testing at the end of the second burn period (hours 2-4), so the final height and weight remained the same. Candle 3 was blown out 60 minutes into the final burn period (hours 4-6) as it was also too short to continue.

For the next step in the analysis, two paired t-tests (a statistical method used to determine the difference in two variables for the same subject) were conducted to determine whether there were any differences in the amount of wax burned or heights across the two conditions – V open to the bottom of V open to the top. To create a data set for this analysis, the difference in height/weight were calculated from the initial measurement to the final measurement. Since candles 3 and 5 in the V open to the top condition burned abnormally (dripped), the data for sets 3 and 5 was excluded. This yielded a single value for each candle in the experiment for candle sets 1, 2, and 4 as shown in Table 10.

Table 10: Change in Height and Weight for Conditions V Open to Bottom and V Open to Top

Δ Height (cm)	V open to bottom	V open to top	Δ Weight (g)	V open to bottom	V open to top
1	14.3	13.9	32	34	32.9
2	14.1	14.7	32.5	34	34
4	14.1	14.9	32.15	32	47

The results of the paired t-tests showed no statistical significance.

Finally, a Wilcoxon signed-rank test (a non-parametric rank test used to compare two populations using two matched samples) was conducted with the null hypothesis H_0 = there is no significant difference in burn behavior between wick with a V open to the bottom and V open to the top. With $\alpha = 0.10$, the test statistics for both height and weight were not less than the critical value, so the null hypothesis cannot be rejected. It should be noted the sample size is still rather small and repeating the experiment with a minimum of 10 sets should be considered.

Summary

Quantitative Data

Based on the change in height and weight of the candles over the course of three burn periods of two hours each, there appears to be no significant difference in the burn behavior of candles with the V of the wick opening to the bottom or the top of the candle.

Qualitative Data

During the burn tests, mushrooming of the wick was evident for candles with the V opening to the bottom of the candle. All candles exhibited mushrooming in the first two time periods and most exhibited mushrooming in the final time period.

Conclusion

The direction of the wick appears to affect the visual burn behavior of candles, but does not appear to affect the quantitative measures of height or weight. It is recommended to repeat this experiment with a larger sample size to validate these conclusions.

Limitations

The limitations of this experiment include:

- Limitations in measuring tools (accuracy of scale or ruler)
- Only examined one type of candle (dipped taper)
- Behavior may change with beeswax from other batches
- Location is not fully isolated
- Some candle were not fully upright, which caused dripping at some stages reducing the valid sample size

Appendix B: Does priming square braid wick affect burn behavior in dipped taper candles?

Hypothesis
Priming square braid wick on beeswax dipped taper candles will affect burn behavior in beeswax dipped taper candles.

Procedure
1. Make 5 pairs of dipped tapers. One candle in each pair will have a primed wick while the other does not. Primed candles are marked with a black mark at the top of the wick higher than the 0.5 cm (¼") trimming mark. This part of the wick will be trimmed off prior to burning the candle.
2. Measure (height, base circumference, and base diameter) and weigh (grams) each candle.
3. Set up candles in holders. Trim wicks to approximately 0.5 cm (¼") .
4. Burn candles for two hours. At each 30 minute interval:
   1. Take one picture of the entire experiment including all candles.
   2. Take a picture of the flame of each candle. Ensure they are clearly identified.
   3. Record burn characteristics (see charts below).
5. Extinguish the candles at the end of the two hour burn period.
6. Cool for at least two hours.
7. Record new height and weight for each candle.
8. Repeat steps 3-7 twice more (total of hree sets of data documenting burn time 0-2 hours, 2-4 hours, and 4-6 hours)

Data
A candles have a primed wick (wick has been soaked in beeswax until no more bubbles are released)

B candles do not have a primed wick

The number denotes the pairs that were dipped together.

For consistency, the V in the wick is up in all candles (final results unknown from the other test at the time of making).

Table 11: Candle Specifications Before Starting Tests

Candle Code	Weight (g)	Height (cm)	Circumference (cm)*	Diameter (cm)*
1A	41.67	18.7	6.5	1.8
1B	39.89	17.5	6.5	1.7
2A	41.28	17.5	6.5	1.7
2B	39.79	17.6	6.5	1.8
3A	44.05	18.6	6.5	1.7
3B	40.29	18.0	6.4	1.7
4A	44.28	18.3	6.5	1.7
4B	41.53	18.6	6.4	1.7
5A	42.40	17.7	6.5	1.7
5B	40.47	17.5	6.4	1.7

* Measurements were taken at the base of the candle

Burn Test 1 (0-2 Hours Total Burn Time)

Test Date: November 2, 2023

Table 12: Burn Behavior for Burn Test 1

Candle	Time	Flame Height	Flame Movement	Mushrooming?	Other notes
1A	30 min	~3 cm	Good	No	Wick exposed ~1 cm
	60 min	~3 cm	Good	No	Wick exposed ~1 cm
	90 min	~3 cm	Good	No	Wick exposed ~1 cm
	120 min	~3 cm	Good	No	Wick exposed ~1 cm
1B	30 min	~3 cm	Good	No	Wick exposed ~1 cm
	60 min	~3 cm	Good	No	Wick exposed ~1 cm
	90 min	~3 cm	Good	No	Wick exposed ~1 cm
	120 min	~3 cm	Good	No	Wick exposed ~1 cm
2A	30 min	~3 cm	Good	No	Wick exposed ~1 cm
	60 min	~3 cm	Good	No	Wick exposed ~1 cm
	90 min	~3 cm	Good	No	Wick exposed ~1 cm
	120 min	~3 cm	Good	No	Wick exposed ~1 cm
2B	30 min	~3 cm	Good	No	Wick exposed ~1 cm
	60 min	~3 cm	Good	No	Wick exposed ~1 cm
	90 min	~3 cm	Good	No	Wick exposed ~1 cm
	120 min	~3 cm	Good	No	Wick exposed ~1 cm
3A	30 min	~3 cm	Good	No	Wick exposed ~1 cm
	60 min	~3 cm	Good	No	Wick exposed ~1 cm
	90 min	~3 cm	Good	No	Wick exposed ~1 cm

	120 min	~3 cm	Good	No	Wick exposed ~1 cm
3B	30 min	~3 cm	Good	No	Wick exposed ~1 cm
	60 min	~3 cm	Good	No	Wick exposed ~1 cm
	90 min	~3 cm	Good	No	Wick exposed ~1 cm
	120 min	~3 cm	Good	No	Wick exposed ~1 cm
4A	30 min	~3 cm	Good	No	Wick exposed ~1 cm
	60 min	~3 cm	Good	No	Wick exposed ~1 cm
	90 min	~3 cm	Good	No	Wick exposed ~1 cm
	120 min	~3 cm	Good	No	Wick exposed ~1 cm
4B	30 min	~3 cm	Good	No	Wick exposed ~1 cm
	60 min	~3 cm	Good	No	Wick exposed ~1 cm
	90 min	~3 cm	Good	No	Wick exposed ~1 cm
	120 min	~3 cm	Good	No	Wick exposed ~1 cm
5A	30 min	~3 cm	Good	No	Wick exposed ~1 cm
	60 min	~3 cm	Good	No	Wick exposed ~1 cm
	90 min	~3 cm	Good	No	Wick exposed ~1 cm
	120 min	~3 cm	Good	No	Wick exposed ~1 cm
5B	30 min	~3 cm	Good	No	Wick exposed ~1 cm
	60 min	~3 cm	Good	No	Wick exposed ~1 cm
	90 min	~3 cm	Good	No	Wick exposed ~1 cm
	120 min	~3 cm	Good	No	Wick exposed ~1 cm

Burn Test 2 (2-4 Hours Total Burn Time)

Test Date: November 3, 2023

Table 13: Candle Height and Weight Prior to Burn Test 2

Candle Code	Weight (g)	Height (cm)
1A	31.10	11.0
1B	28.96	11.0
2A	30.30	10.9
2B	29.08	11.0
3A	33.49	12.0
3B	29.70	11.5
4A	33.78	11.9
4B	30.81	11.9
5A	31.79	11.0
5B	29.94	11.1

Table 14: Burn Behavior for Burn Test 2

Candle	Time	Flame Height	Flame Movement	Mushrooming?	Other notes
1A	30 min	~3 cm	Good	No	Wick exposed ~1 cm
	60 min	~3 cm	Good	No	Wick exposed ~1 cm
	90 min	~3 cm	Good	No	Wick exposed ~1 cm
	120 min	~3 cm	Good	No	Wick exposed ~1 cm
1B	30 min	~3 cm	Good	No	Wick exposed ~1 cm
	60 min	~3 cm	Good	No	Wick exposed ~1 cm
	90 min	~3 cm	Good	No	Wick exposed ~1 cm
	120 min	~3 cm	Good	No	Wick exposed ~1 cm
2A	30 min	~3 cm	Good	No	Wick exposed ~1 cm
	60 min	~3 cm	Good	No	Wick exposed ~1 cm
	90 min	~3 cm	Good	No	Wick exposed ~1 cm
	120 min	~3 cm	Good	No	Wick exposed ~1 cm
2B	30 min	~3 cm	Good	No	Wick exposed ~1 cm
	60 min	~3 cm	Good	No	Wick exposed ~1 cm

	90 min	~3 cm	Good	No	Wick exposed ~1 cm
	120 min	~3 cm	Good	No	Wick exposed ~1 cm
3A	30 min	~3 cm	Good	No	Wick exposed ~1 cm
	60 min	~3 cm	Good	No	Wick exposed ~1 cm
	90 min	~3 cm	Good	No	Wick exposed ~1 cm
	120 min	~3 cm	Good	No	Wick exposed ~1 cm
3B	30 min	~3 cm	Good	No	Wick exposed ~1 cm
	60 min	~3 cm	Good	No	Wick exposed ~1 cm
	90 min	~3 cm	Good	No	Wick exposed ~1 cm
	120 min	~3 cm	Good	No	Wick exposed ~1 cm
4A	30 min	~3 cm	Good	No	Wick exposed ~1 cm; dripped a bit – may be slightly tilted in direction of drip
	60 min	~3 cm	Good	No	Wick exposed ~1 cm; no new drips
	90 min	~3 cm	Good	No	Wick exposed ~1 cm; no new drips
	120 min	~3 cm	Good	No	Wick exposed ~1 cm; no new drips
4B	30 min	~3 cm	Good	No	Wick exposed ~1 cm
	60 min	~3 cm	Good	No	Wick exposed ~1 cm
	90 min	~3 cm	Good	No	Wick exposed ~1 cm
	120 min	~3 cm	Good	No	Wick exposed ~1 cm
5A	30 min	~3 cm	Good	No	Wick exposed ~1 cm
	60 min	~3 cm	Good	No	Wick exposed ~1 cm
	90 min	~3 cm	Good	No	Wick exposed ~1 cm
	120 min	~3 cm	Good	No	Wick exposed ~1 cm
5B	30 min	~3 cm	Good	No	Wick exposed ~1 cm
	60 min	~3 cm	Good	No	Wick exposed ~1 cm
	90 min	~3 cm	Good	No	Wick exposed ~1 cm
	120 min				N/A extinguished

Burn Test 3 (4-6 Hours Total Burn Time)

Test Date: November 3, 2023

Table 15: Candle Height and Weight Prior to Burn Test 3

Candle Code	Weight (g)	Height (cm)
1A	20.27	7.1
1B	17.97	6.5
2A	19.87	7.0
2B	18.28	6.9
3A	22.50	7.6
3B	18.84	7.0
4A	22.85	7.7
4B	19.87	7.4
5A	21.28	7.4
5B	19.71	7.1

Table 16: Burn Behavior for Burn Test 3

Candle	Time	Flame Height	Flame Movement	Mushrooming?	Other notes
1A	30 min	~3 cm	Good	No	Wick exposed ~1 cm
	60 min	~3 cm	Good	No	Wick exposed ~1 cm
	90 min	~3 cm	Good	No	Wick exposed ~1 cm
	120 min	~3 cm	Good	No	Wick exposed ~1 cm
1B	30 min	~3 cm	Good	No	Wick exposed ~1 cm
	60 min	~3 cm	Good	No	Wick exposed ~1 cm
	90 min	~3 cm	Good	No	Wick exposed ~1 cm
	120 min	~3 cm	Good	No	Wick exposed ~1 cm
2A	30 min	~3 cm	Good	No	Wick exposed ~1 cm
	60 min	~3 cm	Good	No	Wick exposed ~1 cm
	90 min	~3 cm	Good	No	Wick exposed ~1 cm
	120 min	~3 cm	Good	No	Wick exposed ~1 cm
2B	30 min	~3 cm	Good	No	Wick exposed ~1 cm
	60 min	~3 cm	Good	No	Wick exposed ~1 cm

	90 min	~3 cm	Good	No	Wick exposed ~1 cm
	120 min	~3 cm	Good	No	Wick exposed ~1 cm
3A	30 min	~3 cm	Good	No	Wick exposed ~1 cm
	60 min	~3 cm	Good	No	Wick exposed ~1 cm
	90 min	~3 cm	Good	No	Wick exposed ~1 cm
	120 min	~3 cm	Good	No	Wick exposed ~1 cm
3B	30 min	~3 cm	Good	No	Wick exposed ~1 cm
	60 min	~3 cm	Good	No	Wick exposed ~1 cm
	90 min	~3 cm	Good	No	Wick exposed ~1 cm
	120 min	~3 cm	Good	No	Wick exposed ~1 cm
4A	30 min	~3 cm	Good	No	Wick exposed ~1 cm
	60 min	~3 cm	Good	No	Wick exposed ~1 cm
	90 min	~3 cm	Good	No	Wick exposed ~1 cm
	120 min	~3 cm	Good	No	Wick exposed ~1 cm
4B	30 min	~3 cm	Good	No	Wick exposed ~1 cm; some dripping
	60 min	~3 cm	Good	No	Wick exposed ~1 cm; no additional dripping
	90 min	~3 cm	Good	No	Wick exposed ~1 cm; no dripping
	120 min	~3 cm	Good	No	Wick exposed ~1 cm; no dripping
5A	30 min	~3 cm	Good	No	Wick exposed ~1 cm
	60 min	~3 cm	Good	No	Wick exposed ~1 cm
	90 min	~3 cm	Good	No	Wick exposed ~1 cm
	120 min	~3 cm	Good	No	Wick exposed ~1 cm
5B	30 min	~3 cm	Good	No	Wick exposed ~1 cm
	60 min	~3 cm	Good	No	Wick exposed ~1 cm
	90 min	~3 cm	Good	No	Wick exposed ~1 cm
	120 min	~3 cm	Good	No	Wick exposed ~1 cm

Table 17: Final Candle Height and Weight

Test Date: November 3, 2023

Table 15: Candle Height and Weight Prior to Burn Test 3

Candle Code	Weight (g)	Height (cm)
1A	9.30	3.2
1B	7.08	2.8
2A	9.06	3.0
2B	7.24	2.6
3A	11.47	3.9
3B	8.10	3.9
4A	11.65	3.9
4B	8.16	3.0
5A	10.38	3.5
5B	8.98	3.0

Results

To determine whether the candles were consistent in behavior, the differences in height and weight of candles in the same condition - primed or unprimed – V open to bottom or V open to top – were graphed (Figures 5-8).

Figure 5: Height Changes Over Time for Primed Wick

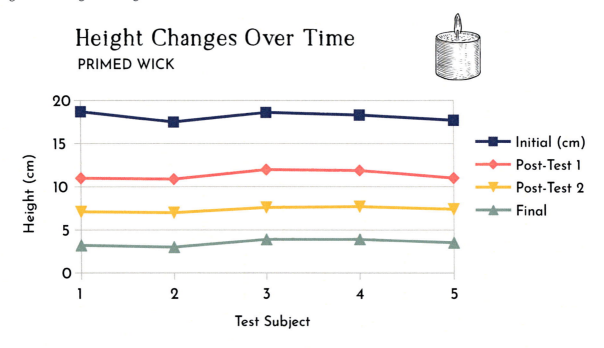

Figure 6: Height Changes Over Time for Unprimed Wick

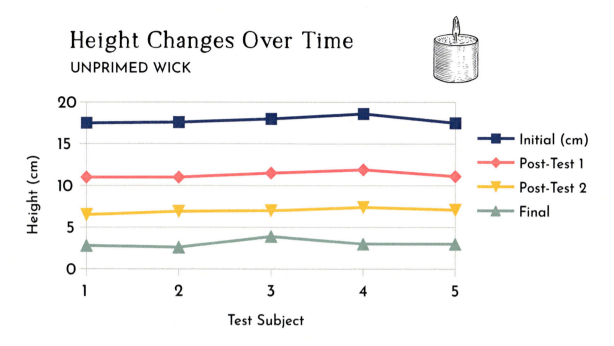

Figure 7: Weight Changes Over Time for Primed Wick

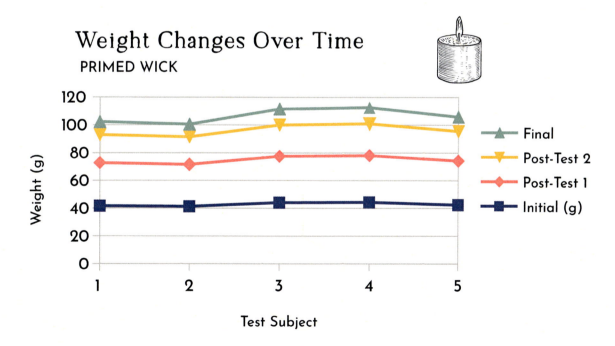

Figure 8: Weight Changes Over Time for Unprimed Wick

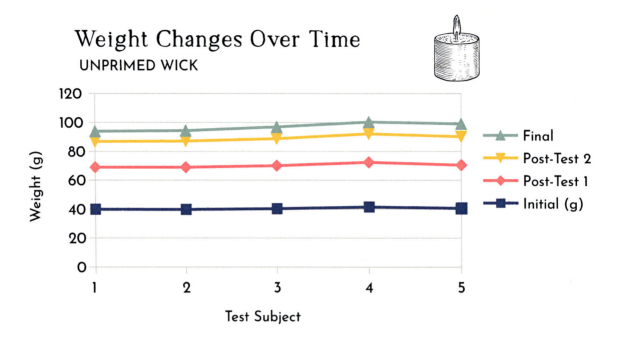

It appears the burn behavior is consistent across both conditions for both weight and height changes.

For the next step in the analysis, two paired t-tests (a statistical method used to determine the difference in two variables for the same subject) were conducted to determine whether there were any differences in the amount of wax burned or heights across the two conditions – primed and unprimed wicks. To create a data set for this analysis, the difference in height/weight were calculated from the initial measurement to the final measurement. This yielded a single value for each candle in the experiment as shown in Table 18.

Table 18: Change in Height and Weight for Primed Wick and Unprimed Wick

Δ Height (cm)	Primed Wick	Unprimed Wick	Δ Weight (g)	Primed Wick	Unprimed Wick
1	15.5	14.7	1	32.37	32.81
2	14.5	15.0	2	32.22	32.55
3	15.5	14.1	3	32.58	32.19
4	14.5	15.6	4	32.63	33.37
5	15.5	14.5	5	32.02	31.49

The results of the paired t-tests showed no statistical significance for both weight and height.

Finally, a Wilcoxon signed-rank test (a non-parametric rank test used to compare two populations using two matched samples) was conducted with the null hypothesis H_0 = there is no significant difference in burn behavior between primed and unprimed wicks. With $\alpha = 0.10$, the test statistics for both height and weight were not less than the critical value, so the null hypothesis cannot be rejected. It should be noted the sample size is still rather small and repeating the experiment with a minimum of 10 sets should be considered.

Summary

Quantitative Data
Based on the change in height and weight of the candles over the course of three burn periods of two hours each, there appears to be no significant difference in the burn behavior of candles with primed wick and those with unprimed wick.

Qualitative Data
During the burn tests, there were no observable differences in the burn behavior between conditions.

Conclusion
Using primed or unprimed wick does not appear to affect burn behavior of beeswax taper candles. It is recommended to repeat this experiment with a larger sample size to validate these conclusions.

Limitations
The limitations of this experiment include:

- Limitations in measuring tools (accuracy of scale or ruler)
- Only examined one type of candle (dipped taper)
- Behavior may change with beeswax from other batches
- Location is not fully isolated

Endnotes

i	Murrell and MacDonald, Beekeeping in Western Canada, 11.
ii	Murrell and MacDonald, Beekeeping in Western Canada, 4.
iii	Murrell and MacDonald, Beekeeping in Western Canada, 96.
iv	Murrell and MacDonald, Beekeeping in Western Canada, 93.
v	Vansell and Bisson, "Origin of Color in Western Beeswax."
vi	Oxford English Dictionary, "Render, v., Sense IV.20.a."
vii	Conrad, "Wax Rendering."
viii	Bogdanov, "Quality and Standards of Pollen and Beeswax"; Fraser, "A Chandler's Guide to Beeswax Candle Making", 3.
ix	Tulloch, "Beeswax—Composition and Analysis," 47-62.
x	Bogdanov, "Quality and Standards of Pollen and Beeswax."
xi	Bartl et al., "Analysis of Efflorescence on Surface of Beeswax Seals."
xii	Bartl et al., "'Wax Bloom' on Beeswax Cultural Heritage Objects."
xiii	National Candle Association, "Elements of a Candle."
xiv	National Candle Association, "Elements of a Candle."
xv	beeculture.com, "Square Braid Wick Sizes."
xvi	National Candle Association, "Elements of a Candle."
xvii	Bogdanov, "Quality and Standards of Pollen and Beeswax."
xviii	Hanif et al., "Essential Oils."
xix	Reyes-Jurado et al., "Essential Oils."
xx	Malle and Schmickl, The Essential Oil Maker's Handbook: Extracting, Distilling & Enjoying Plant Essences, 94, 90.
xxi	wicksandwax.com, "Wicks & Wax Bee Hive Candles."
xxii	Oxford English Dictionary, "Votive."
xxiii	Brown and Diller, "Calculating the Optimum Temperature for Serving Hot Beverages."
xxiv	Bernardin, "Home Canning Step by Step."
xxv	Brown and Diller, "Calculating the Optimum Temperature for Serving Hot Beverages."
xxvi	CandleScience, "How To Conduct a Basic Burn Test;" theflamingcandle.com, "How to Perform Candle Wick Testing."
xxvii	theflamingcandle.com, "How Do I Calculate My Candle Burn Rate?"

Bibliography

Bartl, B., L. Kobera, K. Drábková, M. Ďurovič, and J. Brus. "'Wax Bloom' on Beeswax Cultural Heritage Objects: Exploring the Causes of the Phenomenon." Magnetic Resonance in Chemistry 53, no. 7 (2015): 509–13. https://doi.org/10.1002/mrc.4244.

Bartl, Benjamin, Jiří Trejbal, Michal Ďurovič, Soňa Vašíčková, and Irena Valterová. "Analysis of Efflorescence on Surface of Beeswax Seals." Journal of Cultural Heritage 13, no. 3 (July 1, 2012): 275–84. https://doi.org/10.1016/j.culher.2011.11.007.

Bogdanov, Stefan. "Quality and Standards of Pollen and Beeswax." APIACTA 38 (January 1, 2004): 334–41.

Brown, Fredericka, and Kenneth R. Diller. "Calculating the Optimum Temperature for Serving Hot Beverages." Burns 34, no. 5 (August 1, 2008): 648–54. https://doi.org/10.1016/j.burns.2007.09.012.

CandleScience. "How To Conduct a Basic Burn Test." CandleScience - Candle and Soap Making Supplies. Accessed November 6, 2023. https://www.candlescience.com/learning/how-to-conduct-a-burn-test/.

Conrad, Ross. "Wax Rendering." Accessed April 13, 2021. https://www.beeculture.com/wax-rendering/.

Fraser, Ian. "A Chandler's Guide to Beeswax Candle Making," 2011.

Hanif, Muhammad Asif, Shafaq Nisar, Ghufrana Samin Khan, Zahid Mushtaq, and Muhammad Zubair. "Essential Oils." In Essential Oil Research: Trends in Biosynthesis, Analytics, Industrial Applications and Biotechnological Production, edited by Sonia Malik, 3–17. Cham: Springer International Publishing, 2019. https://doi.org/10.1007/978-3-030-16546-8_1.

"Home Canning Step by Step." Accessed November 6, 2023. https://www.bernardin.ca/en/stepbystep.htm.

"How Do I Calculate My Candle Burn Rate?" Accessed November 6, 2023. https://www.theflamingcandle.com/how-do-i-calculate-my-candle-burn-rate/.

"How to Perform Candle Wick Testing." Accessed November 6, 2023. https://www.theflamingcandle.com/how-to-perform-candle-wick-testing/.

Malle, Bettina, and Helge Schmickl. The Essential Oil Maker's Handbook: Extracting, Distilling & Enjoying Plant Essences. Translated by Paul Lehmann. Spikehorn Press, 2015.

Murrell, D.C., and D.N. MacDonald. Beekeeping in Western Canada. Edited by John Gruszka. Alberta Agriculture and Rural Development, 1998.

National Candle Association. "Elements of a Candle: Wicks." Accessed November 6, 2023. https://candles.org/elements-of-a-candle/wicks/.

Oxford English Dictionary. "Render, v., Sense IV.20.a." Oxford University Press, September 2023. Oxford English Dictionary. https://doi.org/10.1093/OED/1495250556.

Oxford English Dictionary. "Votive." Accessed November 6, 2023. https://www.oed.com/dictionary/votive_n?tab=meaning_and_use.

Reyes-Jurado, Fatima, Avelina Franco-Vega, Nelly Ramírez-Corona, Enrique Palou, and Aurelio López-Malo. "Essential Oils: Antimicrobial Activities, Extraction Methods, and Their Modeling." Food Engineering Reviews 7, no. 3 (September 1, 2015): 275–97. https://doi.org/10.1007/s12393-014-9099-2.

"Square Braid Wick Sizes." Accessed November 6, 2023. https://www.beeculture.com/wp-content/uploads/2015/1½Wax-390x220.jpg.

Tulloch, A. P. "Beeswax—Composition and Analysis." Bee World 61, no. 2 (January 1, 1980): 47–62. https://doi.org/10.1080/0005772X.1980.11097776.

Vansell, G. H., and C. S. Bisson. "Origin of Color in Western Beeswax." Journal of Economic Entomology 28, no. 6 (December 1, 1935): 1001–2. https://doi.org/10.1093/jee/28.6.1001.

"Wicks & Wax Bee Hive Candles," n.d. https://wicksandwax.com/index_htm_files/WicksandWaxBeeHiveCandles.pdf.

About the Author

Lisa Graham, a passionate artisan, nature enthusiast, and a seasoned professional with a diverse educational background, brings a unique blend of skills to the world of handmade beeswax candles. Raised in rural southern Alberta, Lisa's agricultural roots and early experiences working with bees laid the foundation for her future endeavors with beeswax.

Armed with two engineering degrees and a lifetime of experience as a musician and crafter, Lisa seamlessly combines her technical expertise with art and her love for the natural world. Running YYC Beeswax since 2015, she has become a trailblazer in crafting exquisite beeswax candles that not only exude natural beauty but are also practical and eco-friendly.

Beyond her expertise in beeswax candle making, Lisa brings a wealth of experience to the table. She has immersed herself in the worlds of gardening and yoga. Her green thumb as a dedicated gardener and her role as a yoga teacher and practitioner showcase a holistic approach to life that complements her artisanal pursuits.

A sought-after speaker and workshop facilitator, Lisa has shared her insights at numerous events dedicated to sustainable living and handcrafted arts. Her warm and approachable demeanor has inspired many to embrace the therapeutic and rewarding nature of candle making, turning it into a transformative experience.

For Lisa, beeswax candle making is not just a craft; it's a bridge to connect with nature, a canvas for creativity, and a foundation for building a community of like-minded individuals. She invites readers to embark on a journey of discovery, unlocking the secrets of beeswax candle making, and embracing the radiant beauty of handmade illumination in their lives.

Ready to Illuminate Your Creativity?

Get instant access to the video course now and turn your passion for candles into a captivating, hands-on experience!

Unleash Your Creativity with the Beeswax Candle Making Video Course!

Read the book, but craving a more immersive experience? Dive deeper into the art of beeswax candle making with our exclusive video course!

What You'll Get:

- Video Tutorials: Step-by-step guidance for each project featured in the book.
- More on Materials: Explore the intricate details with video content on materials, ensuring you master the essentials.
- Bonus Bee-nanza: Enjoy a curated list of fascinating bee videos – a delightful extra for nature enthusiasts!
- And More: Unlock additional tips, tricks, and insights to elevate your candle making journey.

Why Video?

Experience the magic of candle crafting in action! Our video course brings the book to life, providing a dynamic, immersive learning experience.

Perfect for All Skill Levels:

Whether you're a novice or a seasoned artisan, our video course caters to all skill levels. Elevate your skills and create stunning candles with confidence.

Unlock Exclusive Access:

Enroll today and gain immediate access to a treasure trove of knowledge. Learn, create, and enjoy the therapeutic art of beeswax candle making like never before.

www.artofbeeswax.com/video-course

Join our Beeswax Candle Making Community!

Embark on a journey of creativity and connection with our FREE online beeswax candle making group! Whether you're a curious beginner or a seasoned pro, our community welcomes all enthusiasts.

What You'll Find:

- Q&A Sessions: Have burning questions? Join our interactive Q&A sessions and get expert advice and insights.
- Show and Tell: Explore a gallery of creations from fellow candle makers. Be inspired by the diverse styles and techniques.
- Connect with Peers: Share your experiences, seek advice, and connect with a supportive community of like-minded candle enthusiasts.

Why Join?

- Global Connection: Connect with candle makers from around the world, exchanging ideas and techniques that transcend borders.
- Continuous Learning: Beyond the book, dive into ongoing discussions, tips, and tricks to continuously enhance your craft.
- Celebrate Creativity: Share your latest creations, celebrate milestones, and be part of a community that values every wax masterpiece.

Free to Join:

Become a member today and immerse yourself in the world of beeswax candle making. Best of all, it's completely FREE!

www.artofbeeswax.com/community

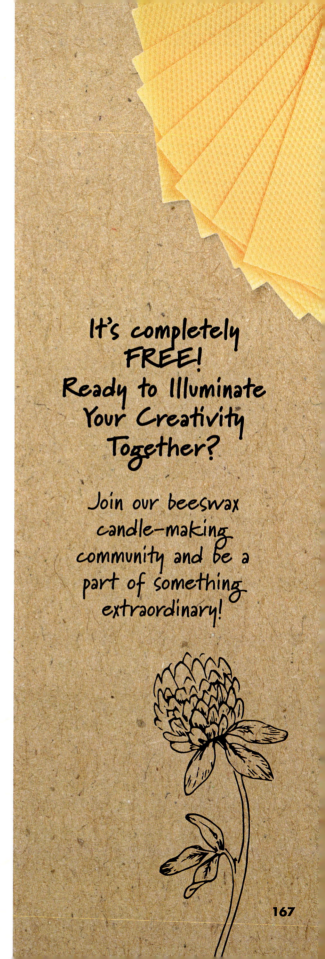

It's completely FREE!
Ready to Illuminate Your Creativity Together?

Join our beeswax candle-making community and be a part of something extraordinary!

Illuminate Your Moments with Custom Beeswax Workshops!

Looking to add a touch of creativity to your special occasions? Book a custom beeswax workshop with us, tailored for various events such as birthdays, bachelorette parties, team building, homeschool activities, and more!

What We Offer:

- In-Person or Virtual Workshops: Choose the setting that suits you best – whether it's a cozy in-person gathering or a virtual event from the comfort of your home.

- Birthday Bliss: Celebrate birthdays in a unique way! Craft personalized candles and create lasting memories with friends and family.

- Team Building: Foster teamwork and creativity in a fun and engaging environment. Our workshops provide a unique team-building experience, and we can integrate any initiatives or company values into the event.

- Homeschool Activities: Add a hands-on, educational element to your homeschooling curriculum. Explore the art and science of beeswax candle making.

Why Choose Us?

- Expert Guidance: Our experienced instructors will guide you through the art of beeswax candle making, ensuring a memorable and enjoyable experience.

- Customizable Options: Tailor the workshop to your preferences, from candle styles to themes, creating an event that reflects your unique vision.

- Seamless Coordination: Whether in person or virtual, we handle the details so you can focus on enjoying the creative process.

www.artofbeeswax.com/book-workshops

Ready to Craft Unforgettable Moments?

Contact us today to discuss and create a custom workshop that suits your event perfectly!

Ignite Your Creativity with Our Creator Starter Pack!

Embark on your beeswax candle making journey hassle-free with our exclusive starter pack! Everything you need for every project in the book, delivered to your doorstep.

What's Included:
- Premium Beeswax: The heart of your creations, sourced for quality.
- Wick Variety: Explore different wick types for varied projects.
- Melting Pots, Tools, and Molds: Essential tools to melt and mold your beeswax with precision.
- Dyes & Scents: A curated selection to experiment with color and fragrance.

Worldwide Shipping:
No matter where you are, we'll bring the art of beeswax candle making to your doorstep! Shop online and let your creativity shine.*

Why Our Starter Pack?
- Aligned with the Book: Tailored to complement the projects in our book, ensuring a seamless and successful candle making experience.
- Perfect for Beginners: Ideal for those just starting their journey or as a thoughtful gift for a fellow candle enthusiast.
- Endless Possibilities: With a variety of materials, the creative possibilities are limitless.

www.artofbeeswax.com/starter-pack

*Please note some countries may have import restrictions on some items in our starter pack. We'll do our best to provide suitable substitutes or alternatives.

Shop Now and Unleash Your Creativity!

Get your exclusive starter pack today and dive into the world of beeswax candle making with confidence!

Craft with Confidence — Shop Today!

Explore our online store now and replenish your stock with the finest materials for your beeswax candle-making adventures!

Restock with Ease — All Materials Now Available!

Replenish your candle making essentials effortlessly with our online store! Whether you're following our book or crafting your unique creations, find all the materials you need right here.

What's in Store:

- Premium Beeswax: Sourced for its quality.
- Wick Varieties: All kinds of wicks for all your projects.
- Dyes: Explore our vibrant dyes to add that extra touch to your candles.
- Molds & Tools: Find the perfect tools for shaping and crafting your beeswax masterpieces.
- So much more!

Worldwide Shipping:

Wherever you are, we deliver! Benefit from our worldwide shipping to keep your candle-making supplies fully stocked.*

Why Shop with Us?

- Aligned with the Book: Our store features materials used in the book, ensuring consistency for your projects.
- Diverse Selection: Discover a wide range of materials, allowing you to explore and experiment with your creativity.
- Convenient Online Experience: Shop from the comfort of your home and have your supplies delivered to your doorstep.

www.artofbeeswax.com/restock

* Please note some countries may have import restrictions on some items in our starter pack. We'll do our best to provide suitable substitutes or alternatives.

Notes

I like to keep a notebook for when I'm creating new recipes.

It may also be helpful to include color swatches in your notebook to remind yourself of the color.

Notes

Notes

Notes

Notes

Notes